# CHEF
## in training

# Kids in the Kitchen

KITCHEN INK PUBLISHING
NEW YORK

**KITCHEN INK**'s *passionate Kids in the Kitchen team of recipe creators, testers, editors, food stylists, photographers, and designers works tirelessly to create products that introduce kids to cooking. Having fun, making memories in the kitchen, and creating a delicious meal is what we are all about.*
*Our easy-to-follow, creative, and delicious recipes—kid tested and parent approved—include both healthy meals and special treats. Adult supervision and safety first are always important in the Kitchen. We hope you enjoy this book as much as we have loved creating it.*

Library of Congress Cataloging-in-Publication data is available.
ISBN 9781943016136

Printed in China

First Edition
28 27 26 25 24  10 9 8 7 6 5 4 3 2 1

**KITCHEN INK PUBLISHING**
**NEW YORK**

Kitchen Ink books may be purchased for educational, business, or sales promotional use. For information, please email the Special Markets Department at sales@kitcheninkpublishing.com

See what Kitchen Ink is up to, share recipes and tips, and shop our store
—www.kitcheninkpublishing.com.

Kitchen Ink Publishing    kitcheninkpublishing

# Contents

# Cooking Tips

- Have an adult helper show you how to use all kitchen tools safely.
- Wash hands thoroughly—at least 20 seconds with warm soapy water.
- Never stand on a chair to reach the stove. Always have an adult help you.
- Be sure your hands are dry when you plug in or disconnect an appliance. When pulling out a plug, always grasp the plug, not the cord.
- When using nonstick cooking spray, be sure to spray over the sink so the floor doesn't get slippery.
- Clean spills and messes as you go to prevent slips and falls.
- Wash produce—fruits and vegetables—before using.
- Always use a cutting board, not the countertop, to chop or cut food.
- Avoid cross contamination—use separate cutting boards and tools when preparing raw meats and veggies.
- Always use potholders when moving hot items to or from the stove or oven.
- Keep your potholders dry. A wet potholder absorbs heat and can lead to burns.
- Always turn pot handles in and away from the edge of the stove to avoid accidentally knocking the pot over.
- Be careful of steam when lifting a pot lid—the steam is hot and can burn you. Always use a pot holder and lift the lid carefully to allow steam to escape.
- Always pick up knives and scissors by the handles. Never put them in a sink of water, where they are hard to see.
- Stir hot mixtures with a wooden spoon or a metal spoon with a wood or plastic handle. An all-metal spoon gets hot; hot enough to burn your hand.
- Always turn off the stove and oven and clean up the kitchen after you are finished cooking.

# Dress Like a Chef

- Wear an apron to protect your clothes from spills.
- If you have long hair tie it back to prevent it from falling into food or getting caught on anything.
- Do not wear shirts with long flowing sleeves that can hang into food or get caught in the flames.
- Wear close-toed shoes to protect your toes from broken glass, hot spills, and dropped cans.
- Always use potholders when putting or removing hot items from the stove or stovetop.
- Wear a smile and make memories in the kitchen.

# Tips on reading a recipe

- Read all the recipe from start to finish. If there is anything you don't understand ask an adult.
- If the recipe you are using references a second recipe look for the page number and turn to that page, read the second recipe and be sure you understand every step to it. Decide which of the two recipes to make first. You may want to make the second recipe first to have it ready.
- Bring out all the tools and utensils you will need
- Bring out all the ingredients you need. If you don't have an ingredient now is the time to get it.
- If you are baking, preheat the oven according to instructions.
- Measure ingredients carefully. Always using a measuring cup or measuring spoons.
- Mix the ingredients by recipe directions.
- Cook and test for doneness as suggested in the recipe. When baking insert a toothpick into the center and if it comes out clean the bread or cake is done.
- Serving size is only a recommendation as people have different appetites.

# Buttermilk Waffles

MAKES 12 WAFFLES

*2 cups all-purpose flour*
*2 tablespoons sugar*
*2 teaspoons baking powder*
*1 teaspoon baking soda*
*½ teaspoon salt*
*2 cups buttermilk*
*¼ cup unsalted butter, melted*
*2 large eggs*

1. In a large bowl, whisk together the flour, sugar, baking powder, baking soda, and salt.
2. In a medium bowl, whisk together the buttermilk and the butter and then whisk in the eggs.
3. Stir the buttermilk mixture into the flour mixture. Continue gently stirring until flour is well combined
4. Turn on the waffle iron and it is ready to use when a drop of water sizzles on contact with the griddle.
5. Spray the waffle iron with cooking spray and pour a ½ cup of batter into each grid of the waffle iron and cook until batter is firm and golden. The amount of batter poured depends on the size of your waffle iron.

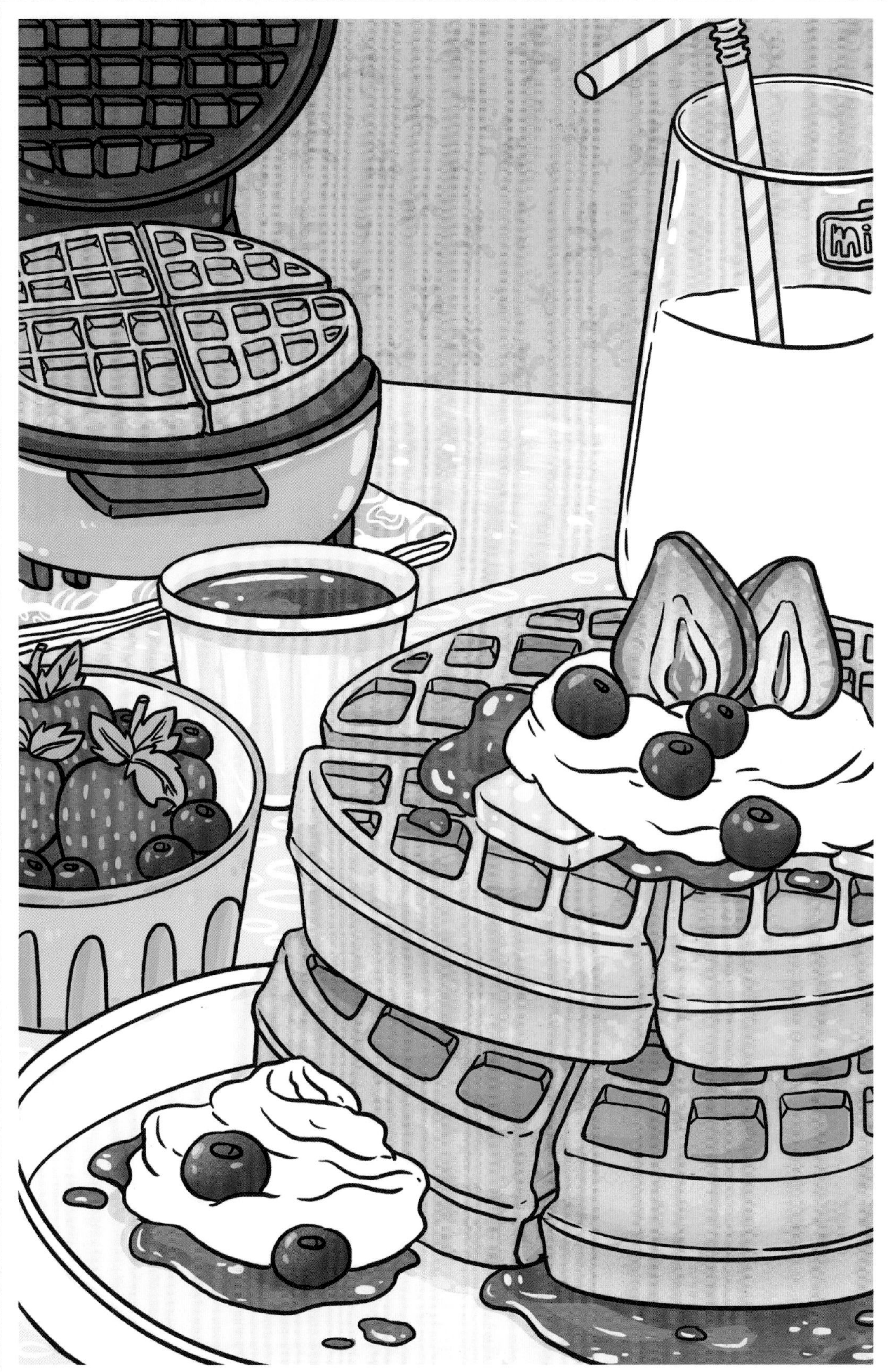

# Egg in a Heart Nest

MAKES 1 SERVING

*1 slice bread*
*1 teaspoon butter*
*1 egg*
*salt and pepper to taste*

1. Cut a shape out of bread with a 3-inch heart-shaped cookie cutter.
2. Melt butter in frying pan, put bread with heart-shaped opening into pan, and break egg into opening. Sprinkle with salt and pepper.
3. When bottom of egg is cooked, flip combination over to toast other side of bread and finish cooking egg, about 1 minute.

# Overnight Oats

MAKES 1 SERVING

*½ cup rolled oats (quick or regular)*
*¾ cup of almond milk (or milk of your choice)*
*1-2 teaspoons pure maple syrup or raw honey*

1. Place oats, milk, and sweetener of choice in an airtight container. A mason jar recommended.
2. Gently shake to fully combine.
3. Refrigerate for 6 to 8 hours.
4. Top with your favorite fruit, nuts, and/or seeds.

# Double Chocolate Pancakes

MAKES 5 SERVINGS

*2 cups flour*
*4 tablespoons sugar*
*1 teaspoon vanilla extract*
*2 eggs*
*⅓ cup cocoa powder*
*2 cups buttermilk*
*2 teaspoons baking powder*
*¼ teaspoon kosher salt*

**FOR THE CHOCOLATE GANACHE**
*3.5 ounces dark chocolate*
*3.5 ounces heavy cream*

1. In a large bowl, add flour, sugar, salt, baking powder, cocoa powder, and mix with a whisk until combined.

2. Add the buttermilk, vanilla extract, and eggs. Mix with a whisk until the pancake batter is just combined.

3. Melt ½ teaspoon of butter on a skillet over medium heat and cook each pancake until bubbles are formed on the top of the pancakes.

4. Flip the pancake and cook for another minute on medium-low heat.

5. Repeat with the rest of the pancake batter and set aside while you make the chocolate sauce for the pancakes.

6. Melt dark chocolate and heavy cream in a medium bowl in the microwave for about 50 seconds. Let sit for 10 minutes.

7. Mix until the chocolate ganache is smooth and silky.Pour the ganache over the warm pancakes.

# Pancakes

MAKES 4 SERVINGS

*1 cup all-purpose flour*
*1 tablespoon sugar*
*2 teaspoons baking powder*
*½ teaspoon salt*
*1 large egg*
*1 cup milk*
*¼ cup butter, melted*

1. In a small bowl, combine flour, sugar, baking powder, and salt.
2. In a medium bowl, whisk together egg, milk, and butter. Add dry ingredients and stir until just moistened. If batter seems thick, add a little more milk.
3. Preheat a nonstick frying pan or griddle on medium heat. Once hot, lower heat and wait 2 minutes.
4. Spray frying pan or griddle with nonstick spray and pour batter on with a quarter cup measure. When bubbles form on top, turn pancakes over and cook until second side is golden brown.

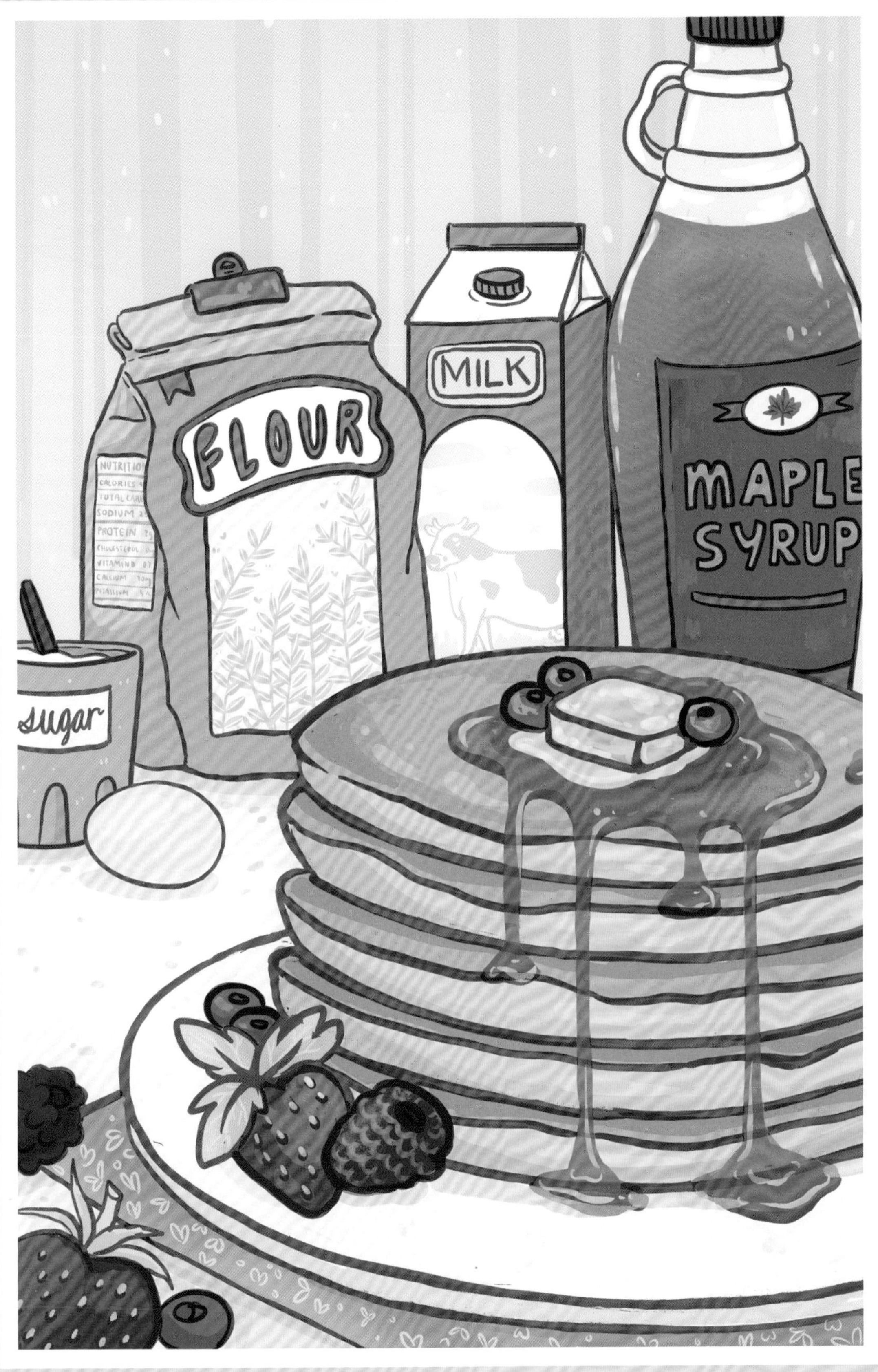
FLOUR
MILK
MAPLE SYRUP
sugar

# Fruit Loops Cereal Bars

MAKES 16 SERVINGS

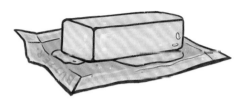

*4 tablespoons unsalted butter*
*5 cups mini marshmallows*
*6 cups Fruit Loops cereal*

1. In a pot, melt butter over low heat. As it melts, add marshmallows stirring frequently until the marshmallows are completely melted.
2. In a large bowl pour cereal adding the melted marshmallow-butter mix. Stir until cereal is fully coated.
3. Put the cereal mixture into a greased pan. Flatten the mix with your spatula until it hardens and cools. Once cooled cut into bars.

# Fresh Fruit Salad

MAKES 8 SERVINGS

*¾ cup orange juice*
*½ cup honey*
*1½ pints fresh strawberries, halved*
*1½ cups fresh blueberries*
*2 oranges, peeled and sectioned*
*1½ cups honeydew melon, scooped into balls or cut into squares*
*⅓ cup mint leaves, chopped*

1. In a large bowl, whisk together juice and honey; add fruit and mint. Chill one hour.

# Yogurt Parfait

## MAKES 5 PARFAITS

*4 cups plain Greek yogurt*
*½ cup pure maple syrup*
*1 teaspoon vanilla*
*½ cup pumpkin seeds, raw and shelled*
*½ cup walnuts, chopped*
*¼ cup chia seeds*
*½ cup flax seeds*
*1 teaspoon cinnamon*
*½ teaspoon cloves, ground*
*¼ teaspoon salt*
*2½ cups mixed berries (blueberries, strawberries, raspberries,*
*    blackberries)—you choose one or all*
*5 parfait glasses or mason jars*

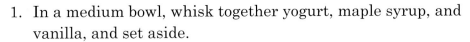

1. In a medium bowl, whisk together yogurt, maple syrup, and vanilla, and set aside.
2. In small bowl, mix pumpkin seeds, walnuts, chia seeds, flax seeds, cinnamon, cloves, and salt.

**To assemble:**
1. Pour ¼ cup of the yogurt mixture into each glass.
2. Top the yogurt with two tablespoons of the nut and seed mixture.
3. Sprinkle two tablespoons of berries on top of the nuts
4. Repeat the layers in each glass until all ingredients have been used
5. Seal glasses or jars tightly with plastic wrap until ready to serve.

# Caprese Avocado Toast

MAKES 2 SERVINGS

*1 avocado*
*Salt and pepper to taste*
*2 thick slices sourdough bread, toasted*
*½ cup cherry tomatoes, halved*
*1 cup mozzarella balls*
*Sea salt, for sprinkling*
*2 basil leaves*
*balsamic glaze, for drizzling*

1. Peel and slice avocado and season with salt and pepper.
2. Place avocado slices on toast and top with cherry tomatoes and mozzarella.
3. Sprinkle with sea salt, garnish with basil, and drizzle with balsamic glaze.

# Brown Sugar Oat Muffins

MAKES 12 MUFFINS

*1 cup old-fashioned oats*
*1 cup whole wheat flour*
*¾ cup brown sugar, packed*
*½ cup all-purpose flour*
*2 teaspoons baking powder*
*½ teaspoon salt*
*2 large eggs, room temperature*
*¾ cup milk*
*¼ cup canola oil*
*1 teaspoon vanilla extract*

1. Preheat oven to 400°F. Grease or paper-line cups of a muffin tin.
2. In a medium bowl, combine the oats, whole wheat flour, sugar, all-purpose flour, baking powder, and salt.
3. In another medium bowl, whisk together eggs, milk, oil and vanilla extract. Add to oat mixture; stir just until moistened.
4. Fill muffin cups two-thirds full. Bake 15 to 17 minutes or until a toothpick inserted in center comes out clean.
5. Cool 5 minutes before removing muffins to a wire rack. Serve warm.

# Blueberry Banana Muffins

## MAKES 12 MUFFINS

*1½ cups fresh blueberries*
*1 tablespoon flour, to toss with blueberries*
*1½ cups flour*
*1 teaspoon baking powder*
*1 teaspoon baking soda*
*¼ teaspoon salt*
*1 cup mashed bananas*
*½ cup sugar*
*½ cup butter, melted*
*1 egg, beaten*
*1 teaspoon vanilla*

1. Preheat oven to 375°F. Line a muffin pan with paper liners.
2. In a medium bowl, toss blueberries with 1 tablespoon of flour and set aside.
3. In a large bowl, whisk flour, baking powder, baking soda, and salt.
4. In medium bowl, combine bananas, sugar, butter, egg and vanilla extract. Add to dry ingredients and mix until just combined.
5. Gently fold in blueberries.
6. Pour batter in equal amounts into muffin cups.
7. Bake 18 to 20 minutes or until a toothpick comes out clean. Cool completely.

# Banana Chocolate Chip Muffins

MAKES 12 MUFFINS

*4 ripe bananas*
*2 eggs*
*⅓ cup milk*
*½ cup brown sugar*
*¼ cup ground flax seeds*
*¼ cup canola oil*
*1½ teaspoon vanilla extract*
*1½ cups flaked oats*
*1 cup all-purpose flour*
*1 tablespoon baking powder*
*½ cups chocolate chips*

1. Preheat oven to 400°F and grease a 12 cup muffin tin with non-stick spray or paper liners.
2. Mash the bananas.
3. In a large bowl, mix together the bananas, eggs, milk, brown sugar, flax seeds, oil, and vanilla.
4. Add om the oats, flour, and baking powder.
5. Fold in the chocolate chips.
6. Fill each muffin tin ¾ full of batter.
7. Bake for 20 to 25 minutes or until a toothpick inserted into the middle of muffin comes out clean.

# Peanut Butter Granola Bars

### MAKES 24 BARS

*1 egg white*
*½ cup peanut butter, chunky*
*⅓ cup brown sugar*
*¼ cup honey*
*½ cup unsalted butter, melted*
*2 cups old fashioned oats*
*¼ cup almonds, slivered and toasted*
*⅓ cup miniature chocolate chips*

1. Preheat oven to 350°F and arrange almonds in a single layer on a baking sheet and bake until lightly browned, about 8 to 10 minutes. Remove from oven and set aside.

2. Spray a 7 x 10 ¾ baking pan with vegetable cooking spray. Lay a 6 x 18 piece of parchment paper in the pan, spray with oil, paper will overlap the sides of pan.

3. In a medium bowl using a hand mixer beat egg white until frothy. Stir in the peanut butter, brown sugar, and honey. Add the melted butter, oats, and almonds. Stir to combine, then add the chocolate chips.

4. Using a rubber spatula spread the mixture into the prepared baking pan, pressing lightly to form an even layer. Bake 15 minutes or until the edges begin to brown. Remove from oven and let cool at least one hour. Cut into 1½ inch squares and serve.

# Lemon Blueberry Muffins

MAKES 12 MUFFINS

*¾ cup all-purpose flour*
*¾ cup whole-wheat flour*
*1 teaspoon baking powder*
*½ teaspoon baking soda*
*¼ teaspoon salt*
*¾ cup plain whole milk or Greek yogurt*
*⅓ cup honey or maple syrup*
*¼ cup unsalted butter, melted*
*2 eggs, lightly beaten*
*1 teaspoon pure vanilla extract*
*2 tablespoons lemon zest*
*2 cups blueberries*

1. Preheat oven to 375°F and grease a 12-cup muffin tin with nonstick spray (or paper liners).
2. In a medium bowl, add the all-purpose, whole-wheat flour, baking powder, baking soda, and stir until combined.
3. Stir in the yogurt, honey, butter, eggs, vanilla, and lemon zest. Gently stir in the blueberries.
4. Divide the batter among the prepared muffin tin, using about ¼ cup batter in each cup.
5. Bake for 18 to 20 minutes, or until golden brown around the edges and a toothpick inserted into the center comes out clean.
6. Transfer to a wire rack and let cool fully.

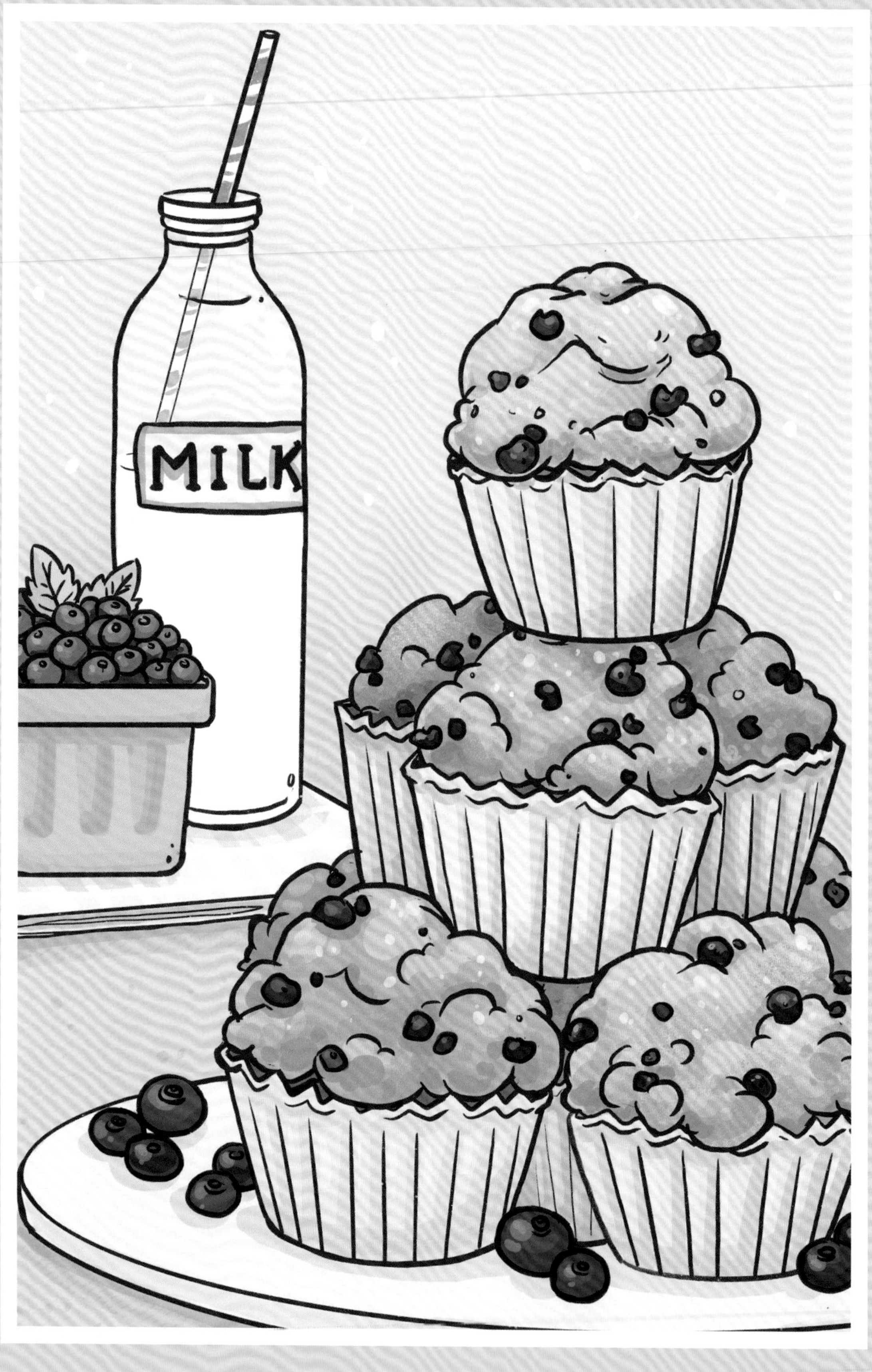
MILK

# Blueberry Muffins

MAKES 12 MUFFINS

*2 cups all-purpose flour*
*¾ cup sugar*
*2 teaspoons baking powder*
*¼ teaspoon salt*
*1 cup milk*
*2 large eggs*
*1 teaspoon vanilla extract*
*½ cup butter, melted*
*2 cups blueberries, fresh or frozen*

1. Preheat oven to 375°F. Prepare a 12-cup muffin tin with nonstick spray or paper liners and set aside.
2. Combine flour, sugar, baking powder, and salt in a large bowl.
3. In a small bowl, whisk together milk, eggs, vanilla extract, and melted butter.
4. Pour wet ingredients into dry ingredients and mix gently until well combined.
5. Gently fold blueberries into batter.
6. Fill muffin cups two-thirds full with batter. Bake for 15 to 20 minutes, until slightly golden brown and a toothpick inserted into center of muffin comes out clean.

# Crepes with Fresh Fruit

MAKES 4 SERVINGS

*1 cup all-purpose flour*
*2 large eggs*
*1 tablespoon sugar*
*¼ teaspoon salt*
*1½ cups whole milk*
*1 tablespoon butter*
*fresh fruit, for serving*
*powdered sugar, for serving*

1. In a large mixing bowl, create a well with flour then add eggs, slowly whisking them into the flour. Add sugar and salt and stir until combined. Gradually add the milk, whisking to combine. Let batter stand at room temperature until bubbly on top, 15 to 20 minutes.

2. In a small skillet over medium heat, melt butter. Drop batter ¼ cup at a time evenly onto pan, using a spatula to evenly coat pan.

3. Cook two minutes, then flip over and cook for an additional minute and remove from pan.

4. Repeat step 2-3 until all batter is cooked.

5. Serve crepes warm with fresh fruit and powdered sugar.

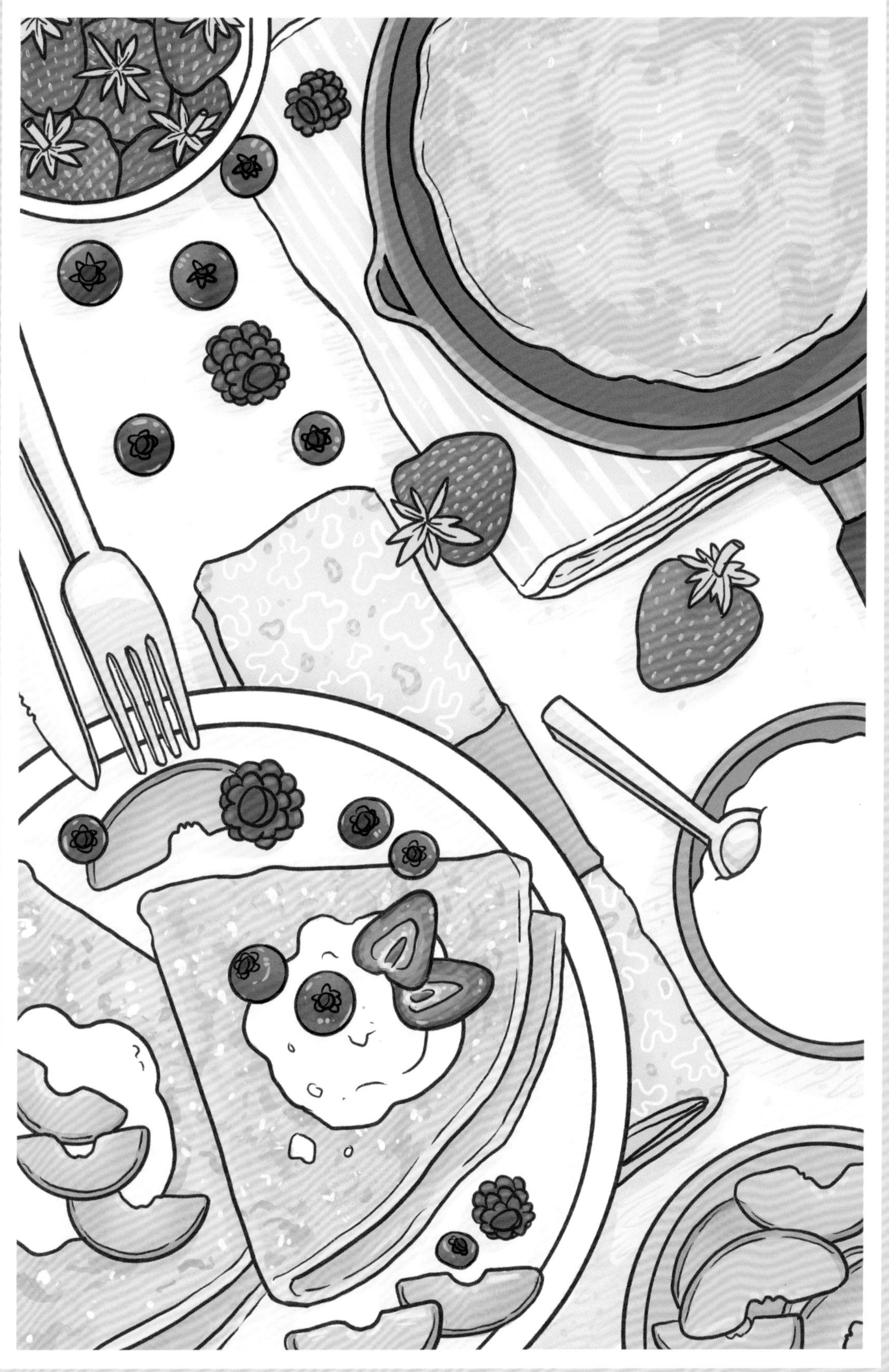

# Cinnamon Rolls

MAKES 12 ROLLS

DOUGH
*1 cup milk, warmed but not hot*
*½ cup plus 1 tablespoon sugar*
*¼ ounce active dry yeast*
*2 large eggs*
*6 tablespoons butter, melted*
*1 teaspoon vanilla extract*
*4 cups all-purpose flour*
*1 teaspoon sea salt*
*1 teaspoon ground cinnamon*

CINNAMON SUGAR FILLING
*1 cup brown sugar, packed*
*2½ tablespoons ground cinnamon*
*6 tablespoons butter, melted*

CREAM CHEESE FROSTING
*4 ounces cream cheese, softened*
*4 tablespoons butter, softened*
*1 cup confectioners' sugar*
*½ teaspoon vanilla extract*
*⅛ teaspoon salt*

DOUGH

1. In a medium bowl, stir together milk, 1 tablespoon sugar, and yeast. Let mixture sit for 5 minutes or until it becomes foamy.
2. Add half cup sugar, eggs, butter, and vanilla to same bowl and mix until combined.
3. Add flour, salt, and cinnamon and mix until dough is formed.

4. Transfer dough to a floured surface and knead for 5 to 7 minutes, until it is smooth and elastic. If it is sticky, add another tablespoon of flour. Form dough into a ball.

5. Place dough into a large greased bowl, cover with a warm, damp cloth, and put in a warm place to rise. Allow dough to rise for about 1 hour or until it has doubled in size.

### FILLING

1. While dough is rising, combine brown sugar and cinnamon in a small bowl. Melt butter separately.

### ASSEMBLY

1. Line a 9 × 13-inch baking pan with parchment paper and grease lightly.

2. Place dough on a floured surface and gently push out air bubbles. Roll dough into a quarter-inch-thick rectangle, about 24 × 12 inches.

3. Spread melted butter on top of dough and sprinkle brown sugar and cinnamon mixture over butter. Press down to make sure it sticks.

4. Roll up dough from long edge, keeping sugared side covered, and cut log into 12 rolls of equal size, approximately 2 inches wide.

5. Place rolls in baking dish, cover with a warm, damp cloth, and let rise approximately 30 minutes or until rolls have doubled in size. While rolls are rising, preheat oven to 350°F.

6. Bake cinnamon rolls for 18 to 20 minutes, until golden brown.

### CREAM CHEESE FROSTING

While rolls are baking, make frosting.

1. In a medium bowl, beat together cream cheese and butter. Slowly add in confectioners' sugar and continue beating until combined. Mix in vanilla extract and salt.

2. Remove rolls from oven. Spread cream cheese frosting over rolls while they are still hot. Serve while still warm and gooey.

# Tater Tot Breakfast Casserole

MAKES 8 SERVINGS

*16 ounces Tater Tots*
*1 tablespoon olive oil*
*1 pound breakfast sausage*
*1 onion, diced*
*1 cup milk*
*½ cup half-and-half*
*¼ teaspoon salt*
*¼ teaspoon cayenne*
*4 large eggs*
*1 red bell pepper, diced*
*1 green pepper, diced*
*2 cups cheddar cheese, shredded*
*1 cup pepper jack cheese, shredded*
*kosher salt, to taste*
*ground black pepper, to taste*

1. Spray a 9 x 13 baking dish with cooking oil and line the bottom of the dish with Tater Tots and set aside.

2. In a large skillet over medium heat cook the sausage and onions. Break sausage up with a wooden spoon and continue to cook for 8 to 10 minutes or until browned. Then spoon over top of Tater Tots.

3. In a large bowl, mix milk, half- and- half, salt, cayenne, eggs, bell peppers, half of both cheeses, salt, and pepper. Pour over the Tater Tots. Cover dish with foil and refrigerate overnight.

4. Preheat the oven to 350ºF and bake covered for 25 minutes. Remove the foil and bake another 25 minutes until the cheese is brown and bubbly. Remove from oven, cut into squares, and serve.

# Breakfast Pizza

MAKES 4 SERVINGS

*cornmeal for the baking sheet*
*flour, dusting for surface*
*1 pound of pizza dough or make your own recipe on pg 91*
*1 tablespoon Dijon mustard*
*1 cup Gruyere cheese, grated*
*4 ounces of ham, thinly sliced*
*1 bunch fresh spinach, stems removed*
*4 large eggs*

1. Preheat oven to 450°F. Lightly dust a baking sheet with cornmeal.
2. Sprinkle flour on countertop, roll out pizza dough into a 16″ circle and place on pizza stone or prepared baking sheet.
3. Spread mustard over dough, then sprinkle with ¾ cup cheese. Top with ham, spinach, and remaining ¼ cup cheese.
4. Crack one egg at a time on top of the pizza making sure to evenly space them out.
5. Bake until crust is golden brown and egg whites are set, 15 to 17 minutes.

# Carrot & Apple Muffins

MAKES 12 MUFFINS

*2 cups flour*
*3 teaspoons baking powder*
*2 teaspoons cinnamon*
*½ teaspoon salt*
*1 cup sugar*
*1 cup vegetable oil*
*3 eggs*
*2 cups raw carrot shredded*
*1 apple peeled and shredded*
*½ cup raisins*

1. Preheat oven to 375°F. Grease or line muffin tins.
2. In a large bowl whisk together flour, baking powder, cinnamon, and salt.
3. In a medium bowl, whisk sugar, oil, and eggs.
4. Stir egg mixture into dry ingredients just until combined.
5. Lightly fold in carrots, apples and raisins.
6. Divide the mixture into prepared muffin tins
7. Bake 25 to 29 minutes or until tops are golden and a toothpick stuck in the middle of the muffin comes out clean.

# Ham and Cheese Muffins

MAKES 12 MUFFINS

*¼ cup butter*
*½ cup onion, minced*
*2 cups flour*
*1 tablespoon baking powder*
*1 teaspoon salt*
*¼ teaspoon pepper*
*¼ teaspoon garlic powder*
*2 eggs*
*1 cup milk*
*1 teaspoon Dijon mustard*
*1 cup ham, diced*
*1 cup sharp cheddar cheese, shredded*

1. Preheat oven to 375°F and lightly grease 12 muffin cups.
2. In a skillet sauté onion in butter until soft.
3. In a medium bowl, combine flour, baking powder, salt, pepper and garlic powder.
4. In another bowl, combine eggs, milk and mustard. Add the sautéed onion, ham and cheese.
5. Stir the wet mixture into the dry mixture just until moistened.
6. Spoon batter into prepared muffin pans and bake in preheated oven for 25 to 30 minutes and a toothpick stuck in the middle of the muffin comes out clean.

# Bacon and Egg Cups

## MAKES 6 SERVINGS

*12 slices whole wheat bread*
*12 large eggs*
*¾ cup cheddar cheese, shredded*
*4 slices bacon, cooked and crumbled*
*salt and pepper, to taste*
*⅓ cup chives, chopped*

1. Preheat oven to 375°F and lightly spray a 12-cup muffin pan with cooking spray.
2. Press each slice of bread into the bottom and sides of a muffin cup and bake for 5 minutes, or until bread cups are lightly toasted.
3. Carefully crack an egg into each bread cup without breaking the yolk.
4. Top each egg with 1 tablespoon shredded cheese, a teaspoon of crumbled bacon, and salt and pepper to taste. Bake about 12 to 15 minutes, or until egg whites are set.
5. Carefully transfer egg cups from muffin tin to a serving plate. Garnish with chopped chives, if desired, and serve with fresh fruit.

# Mini Vegetable Frittatas

MAKES 12 FRITTATAS

*8 eggs*
*½ cup milk*
*1½ teaspoons Italian seasoning*
*¼ teaspoon salt*
*⅛ teaspoon ground black pepper*
*1 cup cheddar cheese, shredded*
*4 ounces goat cheese, crumbled*
*¾ cup yellow squash, chopped*
*¼ cup frozen spinach, thawed and squeezed dry*
*2 tablespoons red onion, finely chopped*
*2 plum tomatoes, seeds removed and diced*

1. Preheat oven to 350°F and spray a 12-cup muffin tin generously with nonstick spray.

2. In a medium bowl, beat eggs, milk, Italian seasoning, salt, and pepper until well blended. Add cheddar cheese, goat cheese, squash, spinach, and onion and mix well.

3. Fill each muffin cup two-thirds full with egg mixture and sprinkle with tomatoes.

4. Bake for 20 to 22 minutes or until eggs are set.
   Run a flat knife around each cup to loosen frittatas.
   Let cool for 5 minutes before serving.

BREAKFAST

# French Toast Sticks

MAKES 32 STICKS

*8 slices thick sourdough bread*
*5 eggs*
*1 cup milk*
*1 tablespoon vanilla extract*
*1 tablespoon sugar*
*2 teaspoons cinnamon*
*2 tablespoons butter*
*confectioners' sugar*
*maple syrup*

1. Cut each piece of bread into four sticks.
2. In a large bowl, whisk together eggs, milk, vanilla extract, sugar, and cinnamon.
3. In a large frying pan, melt butter over medium heat.
4. One by one, dip each bread stick into egg mixture, turning to coat all sides and allowing extra egg to drip off, and place sticks into hot pan. Cook sticks, flipping until each side is golden brown and crispy. Work in batches to avoid overcrowding pan.
5. Transfer sticks to a plate and sprinkle with confectioners' sugar. Serve with maple syrup.

# Breakfast Burritos

MAKES 4 BURRITOS

**AVOCADO-TOMATO SALSA**
*1 large avocado, peeled, pitted, and diced*
*½ cup seeded tomatoes, diced*
*1 small shallot, minced*
*1 clove garlic, minced*
*1 jalapeño pepper, seeded and minced*
*1 tablespoon fresh lime juice*
*½ teaspoon salt*
*¼ teaspoon ground cumin*
*¼ cup fresh cilantro, chopped*

**BREAKFAST BURRITO**
*4 large eggs*
*¼ teaspoon smoked paprika*
*¼ teaspoon salt*
*½ pound spicy sausage (chorizo or Italian), removed from casings*
*1⅓ cups Monterey Jack cheese, shredded*
*four 10-inch flour tortillas*
*vegetable oil*

1. In a medium bowl, add avocado, tomatoes, shallot, garlic, jalapeño pepper, lime juice, salt, cumin, and cilantro. Set aside.

2. In a medium bowl, whisk eggs with smoked paprika and salt. Set aside.

3. In a large nonstick pan over medium-high heat, add sausage and cook, stirring frequently, until browned, 4 to 5 minutes. With a slotted spoon, transfer sausage from pan to a plate, leaving drippings in the pan.

4. Reduce heat to low. Add eggs and scramble until just cooked through. Transfer eggs to a plate.

5. Assemble the burritos: Spoon ¼ cup of the avocado-salsa onto each tortilla, followed ¼ of the sausage, a ¼ of the eggs, and ⅓ cup cheese. Fold in the sides of the tortilla over the filling and roll, tucking in the edges as you go.

6. Lightly coat the pan with oil and set over medium heat. When the pan is hot, add the burritos, seam side down. Cook, covered, until the bottom of the burritos are golden brown, about 3 minutes. Flip the burritos over and continue cooking, covered, until golden, a few minutes more. Serve warm.

# Crustless Broccoli and Cheddar Quiche

MAKES 12 MINI QUICHES

*1 tablespoon olive oil*
*2 cups broccoli florets, cut into bite sized pieces*
*8 large eggs*
*½ cup milk or milk replacement*
*½ cup cheddar cheese, grated*
*½ teaspoon salt*
*¼ teaspoon black pepper*

1. Preheat the oven to 375°F. Generously spray 12 silicone muffin cups with cooking spray

2. In a large skillet over medium heat add the olive oil and the broccoli. Cook for 5 minutes or until tender and remove from heat.

3. In a large bowl, add the eggs and whisk well. Add the milk, cheese, salt and pepper and whisk until incorporated.

4. Divide the cooked broccoli evenly between each muffin cup and pour the egg mixture into each muffin cup.

5. Bake for 13 to 15 minutes, or until set. Cool for 10 minutes on a wire rack, then remove from the cups.

SMOOTHIES

# Orange-Carrot Smoothie

MAKES 2 SERVINGS

*1½ cups carrots, sliced*
*1 cup mango, frozen chunks*
*1 cup vanilla whole-milk yogurt*
*½ cup orange juice, freshly squeezed ½ cup ice cubes*
*1 tablespoon honey*

1. In a blender, combine carrots, mango, yogurt, orange juice, ice cubes and puree until smooth.
2. Pour into two 8 ounce glasses.

# Watermelon Smoothie

MAKES 2 SERVINGS

*3 cups watermelon, cubed*
*10 ounces strawberries, frozen*
*1 banana, peeled and cut into chunks*

1. In a blender, combine watermelon, strawberries, and banana and puree until smooth.
2. Pour into two 8-ounce glasses.

# Green Smoothie Ice Pops

MAKES 6 POPS

*1 banana, peeled and cut into chunks*
*2 cups kale, stems removed and chopped*
*½ cup 2 percent plain Greek yogurt*
*¼ cup pure maple syrup*
*2 small oranges, juiced*
*½ lemon, juiced*
*½ inch fresh ginger, peeled*

1. In a blender, puree the banana, kale, yogurt maple syrup, orange and lemon juices, and ginger until smooth.
2. Divide the smoothie between 4 ounces ice pop molds and place in freezer until pops are hard. A minimum of 8 hours recommended. Remove from freezer and allow a few minutes prior to removing pops from the mold.

# Banana, Pineapple, and Berry Smoothie

## MAKES 2 SERVINGS

*1 cup pineapple juice*
*1 large banana, peeled and cut into chunks*
*1 cup frozen strawberries*
*1 cup frozen blueberries*

1. Pour pineapple juice into a blender and add banana, strawberries, and blueberries. Cover and blend until smooth, about 1 minute.
2. Fill two 8-ounce glasses with smoothie.

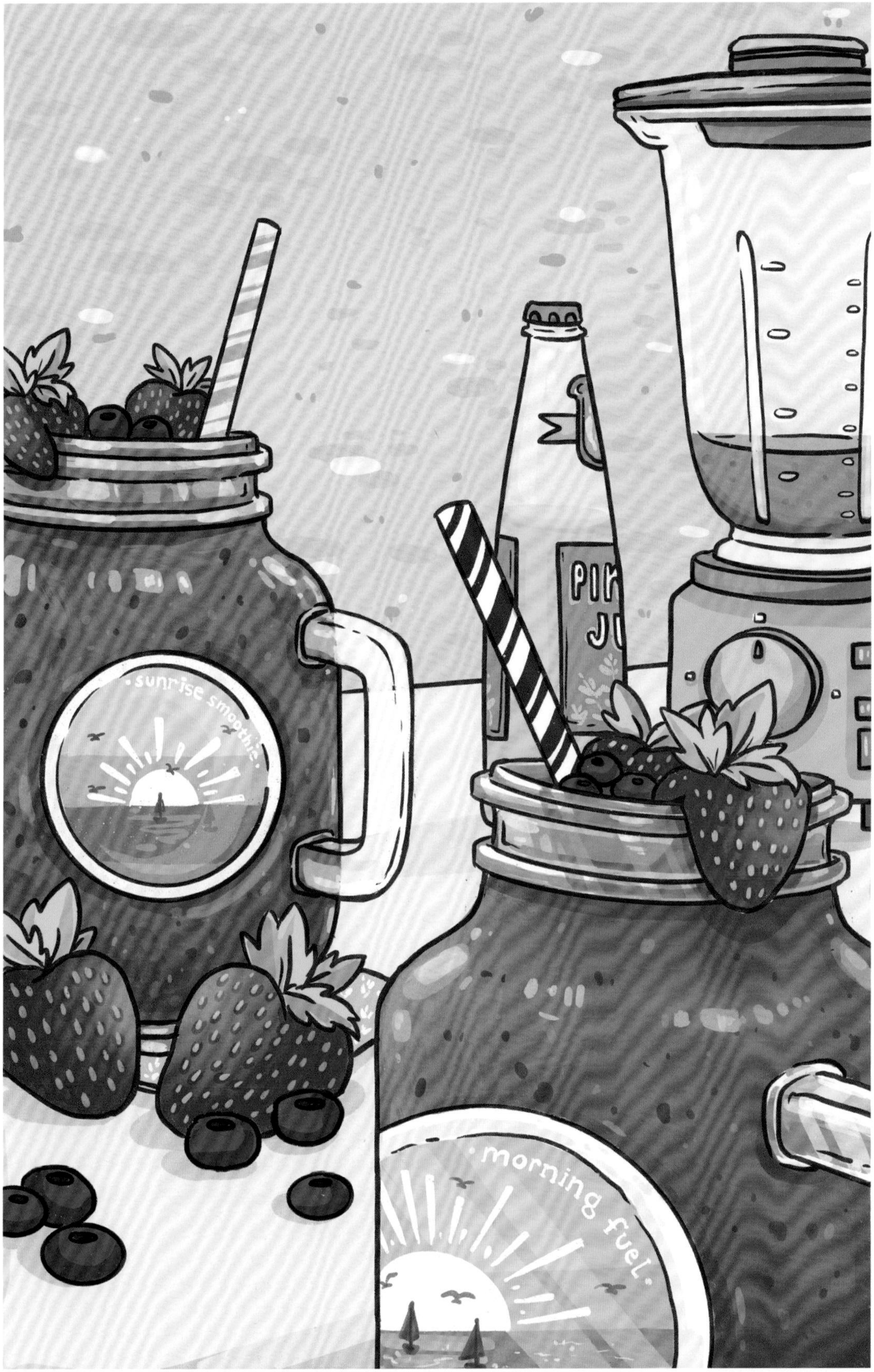
sunrise smoothie
morning fuel

# Raspberry Smoothie Bowls

MAKES 2 SERVINGS

2 cups raspberries, frozen
2 bananas
½ cup nonfat Greek yogurt
½ cup low-fat milk
granola, for serving
toasted coconut flakes, for serving

1. In a blender, puree the raspberries, bananas, yogurt, and milk until smooth.
2. Pour equal portions in two bowls and top with granola and toasted coconut, if desired.

# Peanut Butter Cherry Smoothie

MAKES 4 SERVINGS

½ cup almond milk
2 cups cherries, pitted
½ cup vanilla yogurt
5 ice cubes
¼ cup peanut butter
1 scoop protein powder

1. In a blender combine milk, cherries, yogurt, ice cubes, peanut butter, and protein powder and puree until smooth.
2. Pour smoothie into four glasses.

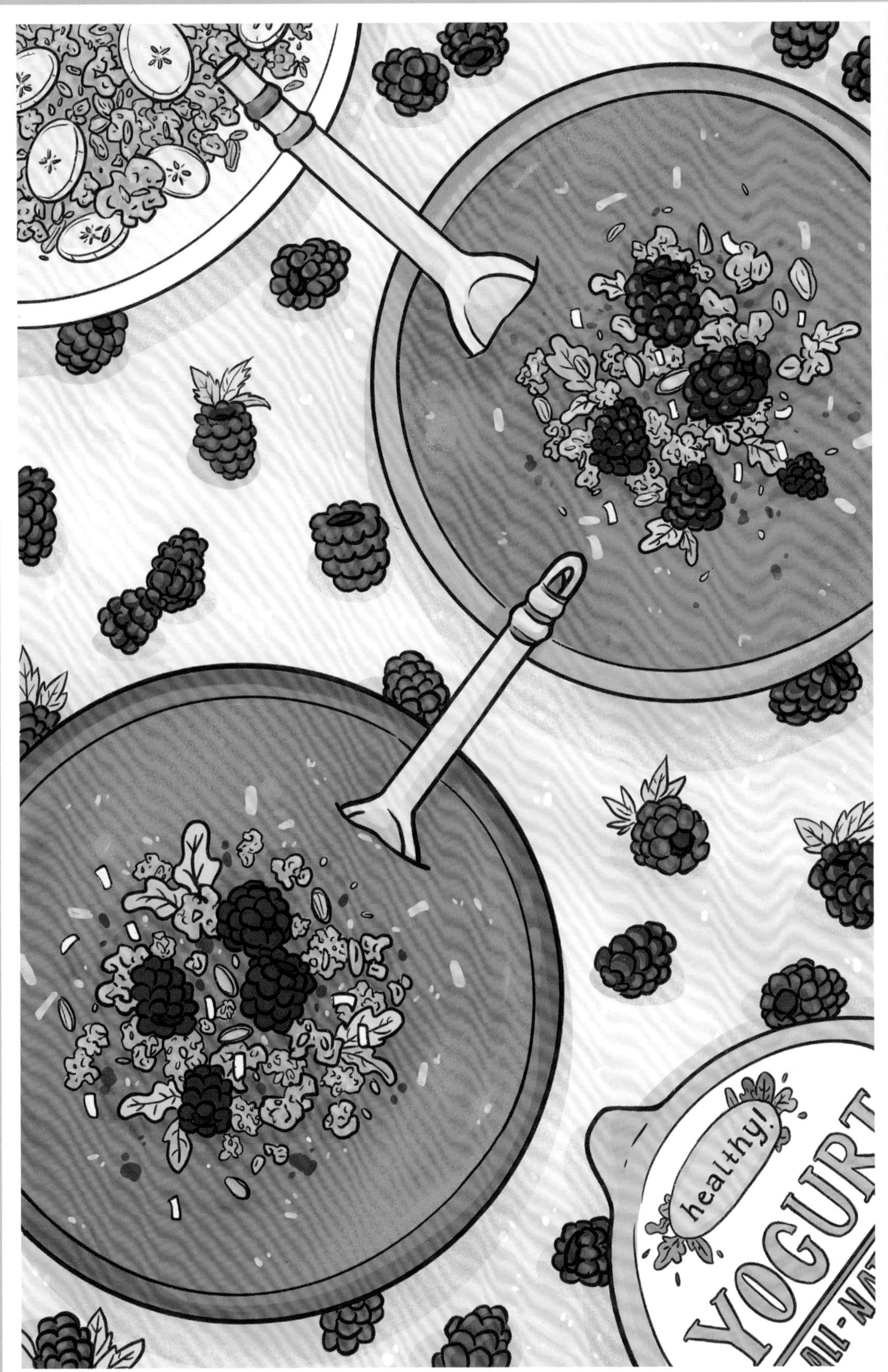
healthy!
YOGURT

# Strawberry Smoothie

MAKES 1 SERVINGS

*2 cups frozen strawberries*
*1 banana, room temperature and cut into pieces*
*¼ cup Greek yogurt*
*1 cup milk, almond milk, or soy milk*
*1½ tablespoon maple syrup, honey, or agave syrup*
*½ cup ice*

1. Place strawberries, banana, yogurt, milk, honey, and ice in a blender. Blend until creamy and frothy, stopping and scraping down the sides as necessary.
2. Pour into a glass and serve immediately.

# Strawberry Watermelon Smoothie

MAKES 2 SMOOTHIES

*3 cups frozen strawberries*
*3 cups cubed watermelon*
*1 banana, room temperature*

1. Place strawberries, watermelon, and banana in a blender and blend until smooth and creamy.
2. Pour into two glasses and serve immediately.

LUNCH & DINNER

# Chicken Noodle Soup

MAKES 4 SERVINGS

*2 teaspoons olive oil*
*1 cup carrots, diced*
*¼ teaspoon garlic powder*
*¼ teaspoon onion powder*
*⅛ teaspoon salt,*
*⅛ teaspoon celery salt*
*⅛ teaspoon turmeric powder*
*32 ounces chicken broth*
*1 cup chicken, cooked and diced*
*1 cup noodles of your choice, adjust the cooking time for your*
*    noodle type*

1. In a large pot, over medium-low heat, sauté the carrots in the oil for 3 to 4 minutes.

2. Stir in the garlic powder, onion powder, salt, celery salt, and turmeric powder.

3. Pour in the chicken broth and turn the heat up to medium-high and bring the pot to a simmer. Add the chicken and noodles, cook for 12 to 15 minutes, until the noodles are cooked through.

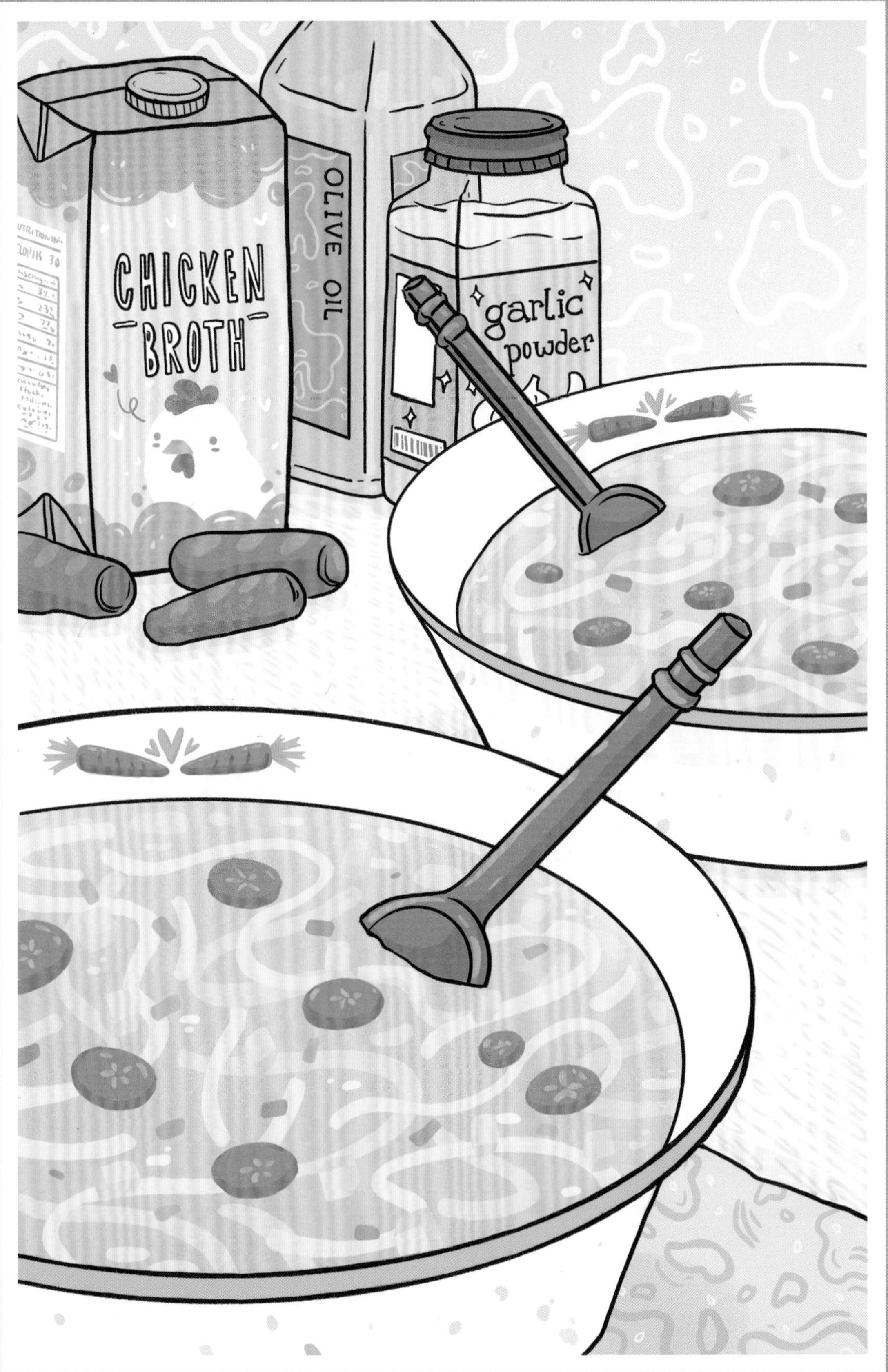
CHICKEN
BROTH
OLIVE OIL
garlic
powder

# Skillet Cornbread

MAKES 8-10 SERVINGS

*1¼ cups coarsely ground cornmeal*
*¾ cup all-purpose flour*
*¼ cup sugar*
*1 teaspoon kosher salt*
*2 teaspoons baking powder*
*2 teaspoons baking soda*
*⅓ cup whole milk*
*1 cup buttermilk*
*2 eggs, lightly beaten*
*8 tablespoons unsalted butter, melted*

1. Preheat oven to 425°F and place a 9-inch cast iron skillet inside to heat while you make the batter.

2. In a large bowl, whisk together the cornmeal, flour, sugar, salt, baking powder, and baking soda. Whisk in milk, buttermilk, and eggs. Whisk in almost all the melted butter, reserving about 1 tablespoon for the skillet later.

3. Using a potholder carefully remove the hot skillet from oven. Reduce oven temperature to 375°F.

4. Coat bottom and the sides of a hot skillet with remaining butter. Pour batter into skillet and place it in center of oven.

5. Bake 20 to 25 minutes or until center is firm and a toothpick inserted into center comes out clean. Allow to cool for 10 to 15 minutes and serve.

# Vegetarian Chili

MAKES 6-8 SERVINGS

*1 large yellow onion, diced*
*1 green bell pepper, diced*
*1 red bell pepper, diced*
*2 sweet potatoes, peeled and diced into 2-inch pieces*
*4 garlic cloves, finely chopped*
*15 ounces can black beans, rinsed*
*15 ounces can kidney beans, rinsed*
*15 ounces can pinto beans, rinsed*
*28 ounces can diced tomatoes*
*20 ounces can enchilada sauce*
*⅓ cup chili powder*
*2 teaspoons cumin*
*2 bay leaves*
*2 teaspoons salt*
*1½ cups water*
*cilantro*
*green onions*
*avocado*

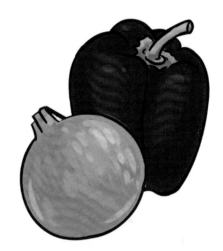

1. In a large pot, heat oil add onions, peppers, potatoes until the onions begin to soften, four to five minutes. Add garlic and sauté for another two minutes.
2. Add the black beans, kidney beans, pinto beans, tomatoes, enchilada sauce, chili powder, cumin, bay leaves, and salt and stir to combine.
3. Add 1½ cups of water to the pot and bring to a boil. Reduce to simmer and cook uncovered for an hour, stirring often.
4. Serve with cilantro, green peppers, avocado, if desired.

# Beef Empanadas

MAKES 4 SERVINGS

**FOR THE DOUGH**
3 cups all-purpose flour, plus
    more for surface
1 teaspoon kosher salt
1 teaspoon baking powder
½ cup butter, cubed
¾ cup water
1 large egg

**FOR THE BEEF FILLING**
1 tablespoon olive oil
1 yellow onion, chopped
2 cloves garlic, minced
1 pound ground beef
1 tablespoon tomato paste

1 teaspoon oregano
1 teaspoon cumin
½ teaspoon paprika
kosher salt
freshly ground black pepper
½ cup, chopped tomatoes
½ cup, chopped pickled
    jalapeños
1¼ cups, shredded cheddar
1¼ cups, shredded Monterey
    Jack
egg wash, for brushing
fresh cilantro, for garnish
sour cream, for serving

1. In a large bowl, whisk together flour, salt, and baking powder. Add butter into flour using your hands until pea sized.

2. In a small bowl, whisk water and egg in a large bowl and mix until a dough forms.

3. Knead dough until smooth. Wrap in plastic wrap and refrigerate for at least 1 hour.

4. Preheat oven to 400°F and line two baking sheets.

5. In a large skillet over medium heat, heat oil. Add onion and cook until soft, then add garlic and cook 1 minute more. Add ground beef and cook, breaking meat up with a wooden spoon. Drain fat.

6. Return pan to medium heat, and stir tomato paste into beef. Add oregano, cumin, and paprika, and season with salt and pepper. Add tomatoes and jalapeños and cook until warmed through.

7. Place dough on a lightly floured surface and divide in half. Roll one half out to ¼″ thick. Using a 4.5″ round cookie cutter, cut out rounds. Repeat with remaining dough.

8. Place about 2 tablespoons of filling in center and top with cheddar and Monterey. Fold dough in half over filling of each dough round. Use a fork to crimp edges together. Repeat with remaining filling and dough.

9. Place empanadas on baking sheets and brush with egg wash. Bake until golden, about 25 minutes.

10. Garnish with cilantro and serve with sour cream.

LUNCH & DINNER

# Pan-Fried Chicken

MAKES 4 SERVINGS

*½ cup all-purpose flour*
*1 teaspoon salt*
*¼ teaspoon black pepper*
*1 teaspoon garlic powder*
*1 teaspoon onion powder*
*2 teaspoons Italian seasoning*
*4 boneless chicken breasts*
*2 tablespoons olive oil*

1. In a large bowl, combine flour, salt, pepper, garlic powder, onion powder, and Italian seasoning.

2. Coat both sides of chicken breasts in flour mixture and set aside.

3. Heat olive oil in a large frying pan over medium-high heat. Add chicken breasts and cook for 4 to 5 minutes on each side, until golden brown on each side and cooked through.

4. Remove chicken from pan and serve with sides, such as Cheddar and Bacon Twice-Baked Potatoes (see page 125).

# Easy Bread

## MAKES 2 LOAVES

*¼ ounce active dry yeast*
*3 tablespoons sugar plus ½ teaspoon sugar*
*2¼ cups warm water*
*1 tablespoon salt*
*6¾ cups all-purpose flour*
*2 tablespoons vegetable or canola oil*

1. In a large bowl, dissolve yeast and ½ teaspoon sugar in warm water. Let stand until bubbles form on surface.

2. Whisk together remaining 3 tablespoons of sugar, salt, and 3 cups of flour.

3. Add oil to yeast mixture, pour yeast mixture into flour mixture, and mix until smooth. Stir in remaining 3¾ cups flour, 1 cup at a time, to form a soft ball of dough. When poked with your finger, dough should bounce back.

4. Flour a flat surface and knead dough for 8 to 10 minutes, until it is smooth and elastic. Rub a bit of oil on dough ball, place in a bowl, cover, and let rise in a warm place until dough has doubled in size, about 1½ to 2 hours.

5. Punch dough down and transfer to a lightly floured surface. Divide dough in half and shape each piece into a loaf.

6. Place dough in two greased 9 × 5-inch loaf pans. Cover and let rise until doubled, about 1 to 1½ hours.

7. Bake at 375°F until golden brown, approximately 30 to 35 minutes. If bread sounds hollow when tapped, it is done.

8. Remove from pans and cool on a wire rack.

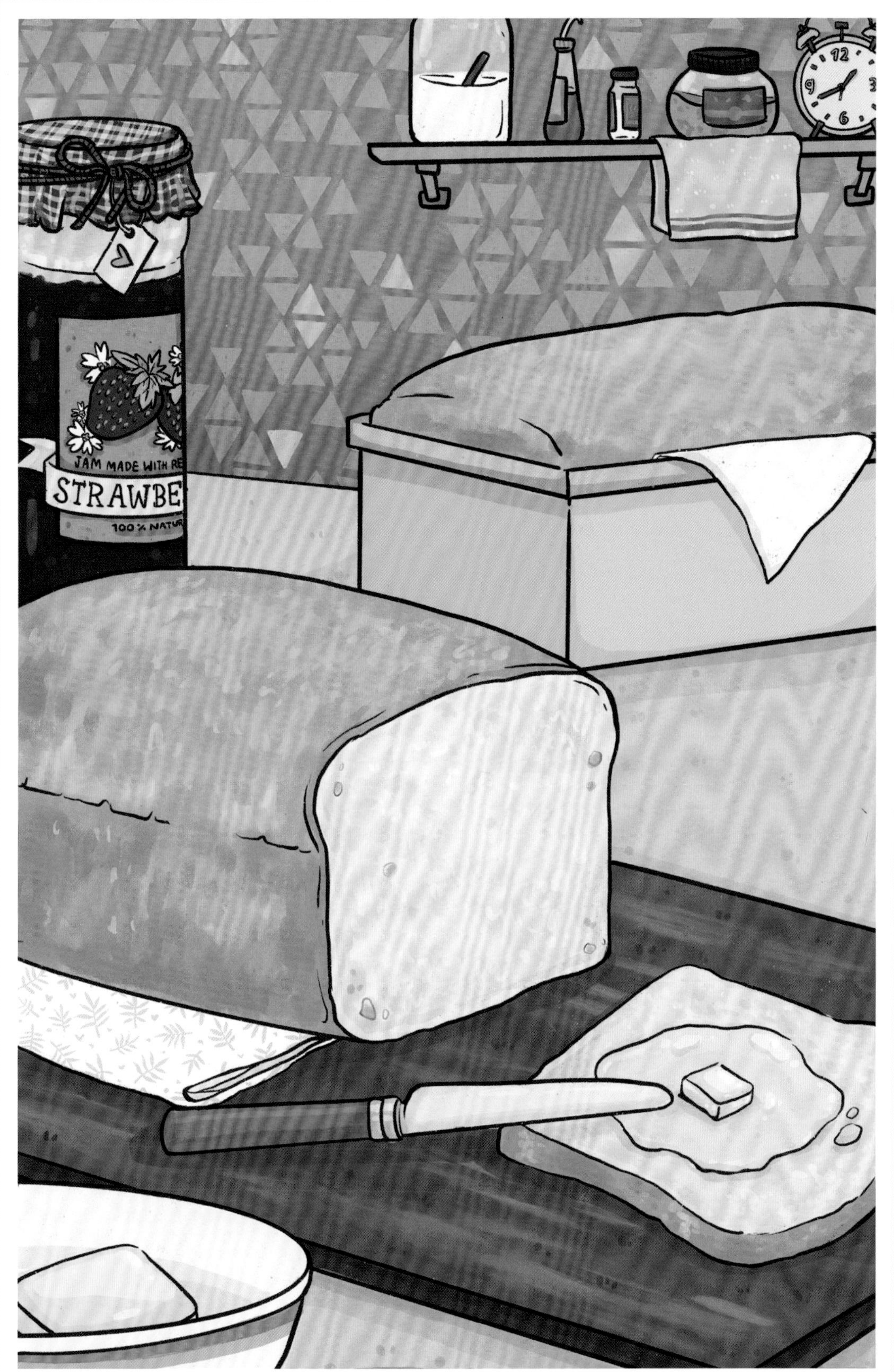
JAM MADE WITH RE
STRAWBE
100% NATUR

# Carrot and Tomato Soup

MAKES 6 CUPS

*7 medium carrots, peeled and chopped*
*2 tablespoons butter*
*2 teaspoons salt*
*2 cups water*
*1 28-ounce can of whole peeled tomatoes*
*⅓ cup cream*
*¼ teaspoon ground black pepper*

**OPTIONAL TOPPINGS**
*crispy onions*
*basil*

1. Put carrots in a large saucepan with 1 tablespoon butter, salt, and water and bring to a boil.
2. Reduce heat to simmer, add tomatoes, and cook for approximately 20 minutes. Remove from heat and let cool.
3. Carefully pour contents of saucepan into a blender and blend until smooth.
4. Return soup to saucepan, add cream, pepper, and remaining butter, and reheat.
5. Pour soup into bowls and top with crispy onions or basil.

# Tofu Vegetable Bowls

MAKES 4 SERVINGS

*2 cups brown rice, uncooked*
*1 block extra-firm tofu*
*1½ tablespoons cornstarch*
*1 cup sweet potatoes, chopped*
*1 cup carrots, chopped*
*1 cup broccoli, chopped*
*1 cup brussels sprouts,*
*    chopped*
*1 cup green bell peppers,*
*    chopped*
*1 cup mushrooms, chopped*
*1 tablespoon olive oil*
*crushed peanuts and sliced*
*    green onions, to top bowls,*
*    if desired*

**EASY PEANUT SAUCE**
*½ cup peanut butter*
*2 tablespoons tamari*
*3 tablespoons ginger, grated*
*1 clove garlic, grated*
*2 tablespoons rice vinegar*
*1 tablespoon sesame oil*
*2 tablespoons maple syrup*
*6 tablespoons water*

1.  Place tofu on a plate between paper towels (or a clean kitchen cloth). Set a heavy object, such as a cast iron pan or heavy pot, on top to drain excess liquid from tofu approx. 1 hour.

2.  Prepare brown rice according to package directions.

3.  Preheat oven to 400°F and line two baking sheets with parchment paper or silicone baking mats.

4.  Once tofu is pressed, cut into cubes. Toss cubes in cornstarch and arrange in a single layer on one of the baking sheets.

5.  In a medium bowl, add potatoes, carrots, broccoli, brussels sprouts, and toss with olive oil, and arrange in a single layer on the second baking sheet.

6.  Bake tofu and vegetables for 20 to 30 minutes or until tofu is lightly browned and crisp around the edges and vegetables are crisp-tender. Add more delicate quick-cooking vegetables such as mushrooms and peppers in the last ten minutes.

7. While tofu and vegetables are baking, in a medium bowl add ½ cup peanut butter, tamari, brown sugar, rice vinegar and garlic. Add tablespoons of water to thin out sauce if necessary.

8. Place a portion of rice in each bowl. Top with tofu and vegetables, drizzle Peanut Sauce on top. Top with crushed peanuts and green onion if desired.

# Macaroni and Cheese

## MAKES 12 SERVINGS

*16 ounces (1 pound) elbow*
*  macaroni pasta*
*6 tablespoons butter*
*⅓ cup flour*
*3 cups milk*
*12 ounces cheddar cheese, or*
*  cheese of your choice*
*¾ teaspoon salt*
*¼ teaspoon pepper*

TOPPING
*2 tablespoons butter, melted*
*4 tablespoons dry bread*
*  crumbs*
*salt*
*pepper*

1. Cook pasta according to directions on package and drain.
2. Preheat oven to 375°F. Lightly grease a 2-quart casserole dish.
3. In a medium saucepan, melt all butter over medium heat. Set aside 2 tablespoons for topping mixture. Stir in flour and slowly add milk, stirring constantly while bringing to a boil.
4. Turn off burner and mix in cheese, salt, and pepper, stirring until cheese is melted. Add macaroni and mix well. Pour into casserole dish.
5. In a small bowl, combine 2 tablespoons melted butter, bread crumbs, and a dash of salt and pepper. Sprinkle over macaroni and cheese.
6. Bake for 30 minutes. Remove from oven and let cool prior to serving.

# Sloppy Joes

MAKES 6 SERVINGS

1 teaspoon olive oil
1 pound ground beef
1 small onion, diced
½ red bell pepper, diced
½ green bell pepper, diced
1 small zucchini, diced
3 cloves garlic, minced
1 tablespoon tomato paste
⅔ cup ketchup

⅓ cup water
1 tablespoon brown sugar
1 teaspoon yellow mustard
¾ teaspoon chili powder
½ teaspoon Worcestershire sauce
½ teaspoon salt
¼ teaspoon black pepper
6 rolls, for serving

1. In a medium frying pan, heat oil over medium-high heat and add ground beef. Cook beef until browned, using wooden spoon to break it apart. Drain beef in a colander and set aside.

2. In same frying pan, combine onion, bell peppers, and zucchini. Cook until vegetables are tender, approximately 5 minutes. Add garlic and cook for 1 minute. Put beef back in pan, add tomato paste, and mix well.

3. Stir in ketchup, water, brown sugar, mustard, chili powder, Worcestershire sauce, salt, and black pepper.

4. Cook over medium heat for 10 to 15 minutes, until mixture has thickened. Remove from heat and serve on rolls.

LUNCH & DINNER

# Sweet & Easy Corn on the Cob

MAKES 6 SERVINGS

*2 tablespoons sugar*
*1 tablespoon lemon juice*
*6 ears corn on the cob, husks and silk removed*

1. Fill a large pot about three-quarters full of water and bring to a boil.
2. Stir in sugar and lemon juice, dissolving sugar.
3. Gently place ears of corn into boiling water, cover the pot, turn off the heat, and let corn cook in the hot water until tender, about 10 minutes.
4. Using tongs, carefully remove ears of corn from the pot.

# Spring Salad with Berries and Bacon

MAKES 6 SERVINGS

*2 tablespoons red wine vinegar*
*1 tablespoon finely chopped shallot*
*1½ teaspoons honey*
*½ teaspoon Dijon mustard*
*3 cups sliced strawberries, divided*
*¾ teaspoon kosher salt, divided*
*¼ cup extra-virgin olive oil*
*5 cups baby spring salad mix*
*4 ounces feta cheese, crumbled*
*1 medium shallot, thinly sliced*
*1 cup yellow cherry tomatoes, halved*
*8 bacon slices, cooked and chopped*

1. TO MAKE VINAIGRETTE DRESSING: In a blender add red wine vinegar, shallot, honey, Dijon mustard, 1 cup of strawberries, and ¼ of salt. Blend until smooth (approx. 30 seconds). Add in oil, blending until combined.

2. On a large platter arrange spring mix and top with feta, shallots, tomatoes, bacon, and remaining 2 cups of strawberries and ½ teaspoons salt. Drizzle dressing over salad, serve immediately.

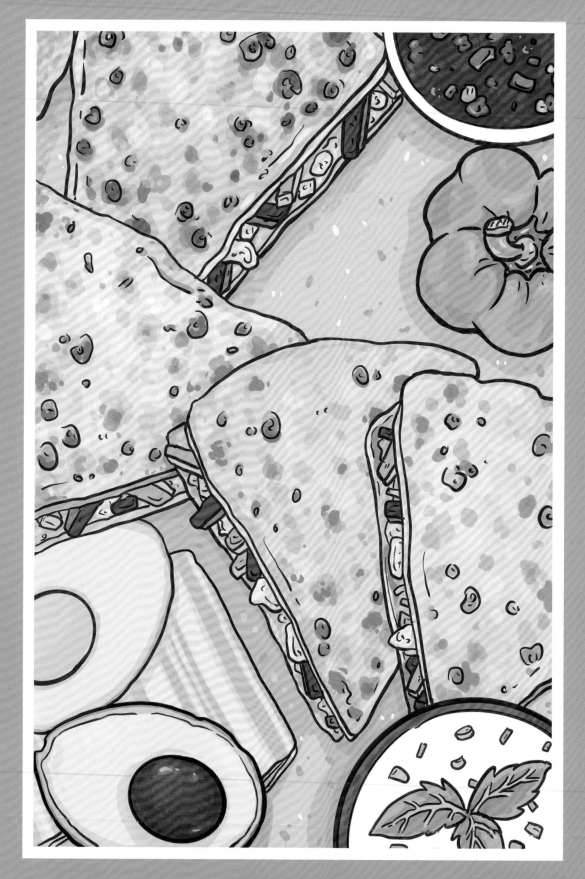

LUNCH & DINNER

# Chicken Quesadillas

MAKES 4 QUESADILLAS

*2 tablespoons olive oil*
*1 green pepper, washed and*
*  sliced*
*1 red pepper, washed and*
*  sliced*
*½ red onion, thinly sliced*
*salt and pepper to taste*
*1 package (2 tablespoons)*
*  taco seasoning*
*1 pound boneless chicken,*
*  sliced into strips*

*8 medium flour tortillas*
*2 cups Monterey Jack cheese,*
*  shredded*
*2 cups cheddar cheese,*
*  shredded*

**TOPPINGS**
*1 avocado, sliced*
*2 green onions, thinly sliced*
*sour cream*
*salsa*

1. In a large frying pan, heat 1 tablespoon olive oil over medium-high heat. Add peppers and onion and season with salt and pepper. Cook until soft, approximately 5 minutes, and transfer to a plate.

2. Pour taco seasoning into a small bowl and coat chicken on both sides with seasoning. Add 1 tablespoon oil to frying pan, cook chicken until golden brown and cooked through, and transfer to a plate.

3. Put 1 tortilla in frying pan, brown lightly on both sides, and top with one-fourth each of two cheeses, pepper and onion mixture, and chicken. Place second tortilla on top and cook 3 minutes per side, flipping stack over like a pancake. Repeat to cook all four quesadillas.

4. Slice each quesadilla into four triangles and serve with toppings.

# Corn Dogs

MAKES 4 CORN DOGS

*4 cups vegetable oil for frying*
*¾ cup yellow cornmeal*
*¾ cup all-purpose flour*
*1½ teaspoons baking powder*
*½ teaspoon baking soda*
*2 teaspoons sugar*
*½ teaspoon salt*
*⅛ teaspoon nutmeg*
*1 cup buttermilk*

*2 eggs*
*4 hot dogs*
*4 wooden skewers*
*all-purpose flour for coating*

TOPPINGS
*ketchup*
*mustard*

1. With assistance of an adult, pour oil into a large heavy saucepan and heat to 375°F.
2. To make batter, in a medium bowl, combine cornmeal, flour, baking powder, baking soda, sugar, salt, and nutmeg.
3. In a small bowl, whisk together buttermilk and eggs. Mix wet ingredients into dry ingredients until no streaks of flour remain, but leave lumps in batter. Transfer batter to a tall glass.
4. Roll each hot dog in flour to coat, shaking off excess flour, and insert skewer lengthwise into middle of hot dog.
5. Dip hot dog into tall glass of batter to cover whole hot dog. With assistance of an adult, put battered hot dog straight into hot oil for about 3 minutes on each side. Depending on size of pot, cook up to three at a time. Corn dogs are ready when batter is cooked to a golden brown.
6. Serve corn dogs with ketchup and mustard.

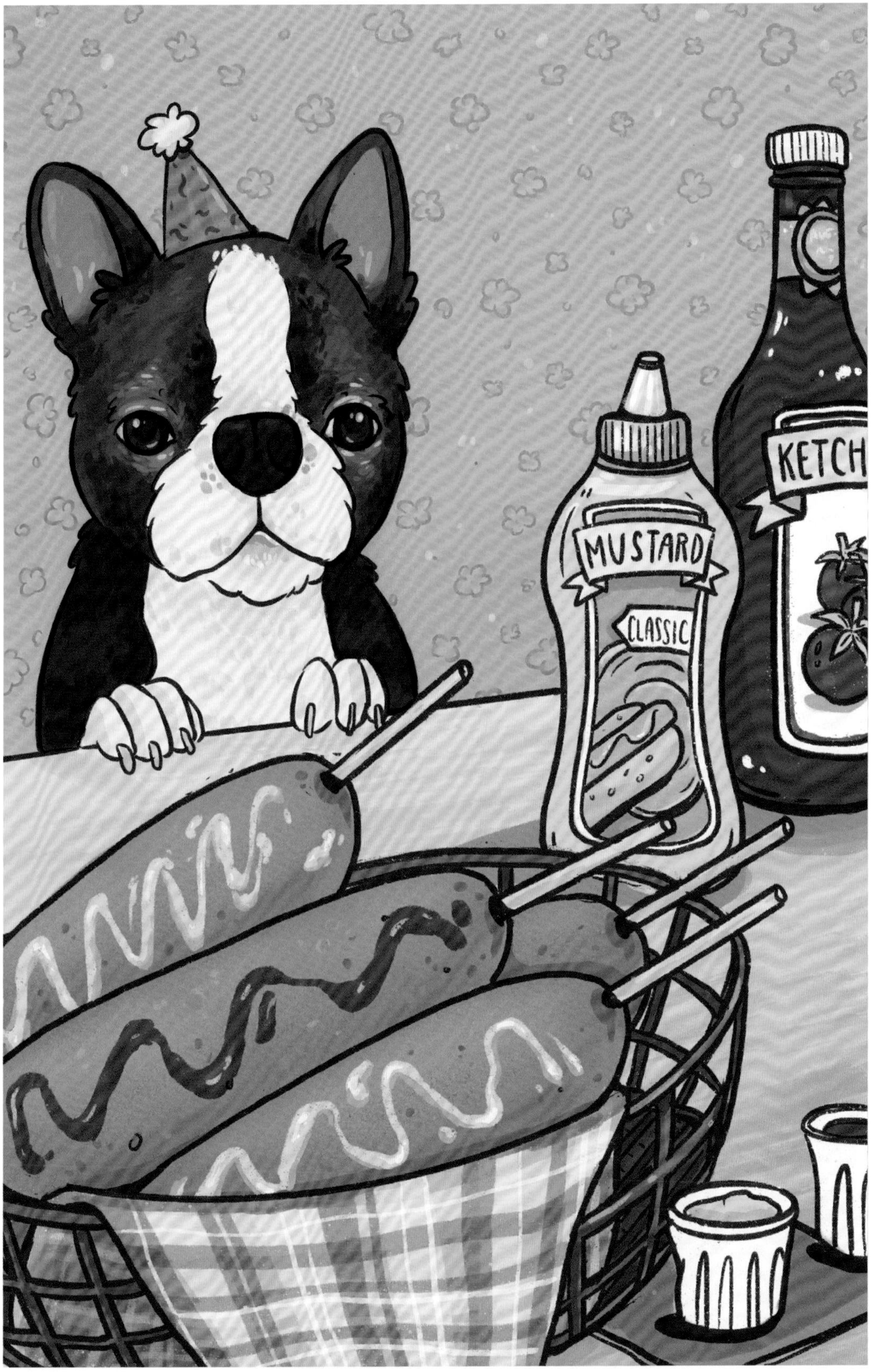

MUSTARD
CLASSIC
KETCH

# Lasagna Roll Ups

## MAKES 12 ROLL UPS

*12 uncooked lasagna noodles*
*2 large eggs, lightly beaten*
*10 ounces frozen chopped spinach, thawed and squeezed dry*
*2½ cups whole-milk ricotta cheese*
*2½ cups shredded part-skim mozzarella cheese*
*½ cup, grated Parmesan cheese*
*¼ teaspoon salt*
*¼ teaspoon pepper*
*¼ teaspoon ground nutmeg*
*24 ounces meatless pasta sauce*

1. Preheat oven to 375°F.
2. Cook noodles according to package directions; drain.
3. In a medium bowl mix egg, spinach, ricotta cheese, mozzarella cheese, parmesan cheese, salt, pepper, and nutmeg.
4. Pour 1 cup pasta sauce into an ungreased 13x9-in. baking dish.
5. Spread ⅓ cup cheese mixture over each noodle; roll up and place over sauce, seam side down. Top with remaining sauce.
6. Bake, covered, 20 minutes. Uncover; bake until heated through, 5 to 10 more minutes.

# Chicken and Rice Casserole

MAKES 4 SERVINGS

*4 boneless chicken breasts*
*salt and pepper*
*1 cup long grain white rice, uncooked*
*1 2-ounce package onion soup mix*
*1 10-ounce can cream of mushroom soup, condensed*
*1½ cups water*

1. Preheat oven to 325°F. Spray a 9 × 13-inch baking dish with nonstick spray.
2. Arrange chicken breasts in baking dish and sprinkle with salt and pepper.
3. Spread uncooked rice over chicken. Sprinkle with onion soup mix.
4. Combine mushroom soup and water and pour over chicken.
5. Cover and bake for 1 hour and 15 minutes, or until rice is tender.

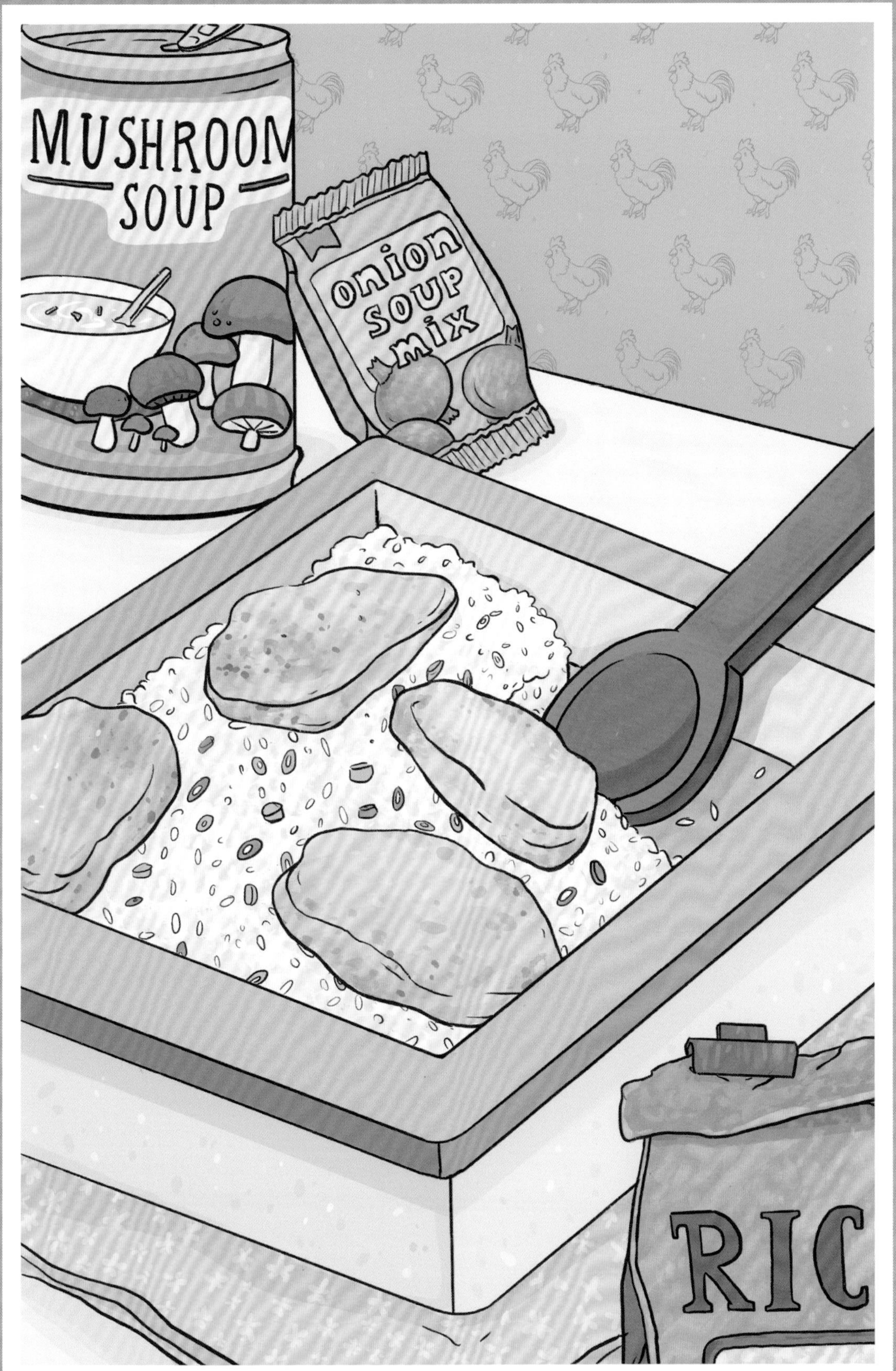
MUSHROOM
SOUP
onion
soup
mix
RIC

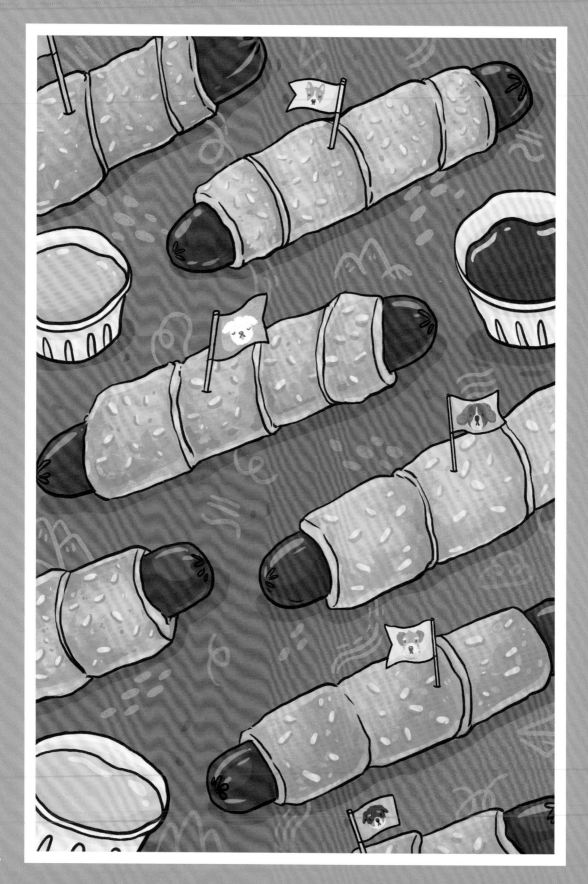

# Hot Dogs Wrapped in Puff Pastry

MAKES 8 HOT DOGS

*16 ounces package of hot dogs*
*10 ounces puff pastry*
*4 tablespoons light mayonnaise*
*1 teaspoon yellow mustard*
*½ teaspoon garlic powder*
*egg white*
*sesame seeds, optional*

1. Preheat oven to 350°F and grease a baking sheet.
2. Lay a sheet of pastry dough down and coat with mayo, mustard, and garlic powder.
3. Wrap dough around each hot dog.
4. Coat the dough with egg wash and sprinkle the dough with sesame seeds.
5. Bake until dough is golden brown, 20 to 22 minutes.

# Baked Beans

MAKES 6-8 SERVINGS

*8 ounces bacon (7 to 8 slices), cut into ½ inch pieces*
*1 medium onion, finely chopped*
*5 garlic cloves, minced*
*2 tablespoons brown sugar*
*⅓ cup molasses*
*one 15 ounce can diced tomatoes*
*⅓ cup ketchup*
*2 tablespoons Worcestershire Sauce*
*2 tablespoons yellow mustard*
*2 teaspoons paprika*
*2 bay leaves*
*½ teaspoon black pepper*
*½ teaspoon cloves, ground*
*1 teaspoon kosher salt*
*three 15 ounce cans navy beans, drained*

1. Heat oven to 325°F.
2. Heat a 6-quart Dutch oven over medium heat. Add bacon and cook until crisp, 7 to 10 minutes. Transfer bacon to a bowl using a slotted spoon.
3. Add onions and garlic to bacon fat in the pot and sauté until soft and translucent, about 5 minutes. Add brown sugar, molasses, tomatoes, ketchup, Worcestershire sauce, mustard, paprika, bay leaves, pepper, cloves, salt, navy beans, and reserved bacon to the pot.
4. Over medium-high heat, bring mixture to a simmer stirring frequently. Cover pot with lid and transfer to the oven. Bake until sauce has thickened, 45 to 55 minutes. Check beans and stir once halfway through cooking time.
5. Let beans rest out of the oven for 10 minutes before serving. Serve beans right from the Dutch oven to keep them warm, the pot will hold the heat. Garnish with extra crisped bacon if desired.

# Creamy Coleslaw

MAKES 6 SERVINGS

*1 small head green cabbage, quartered, cored, and shredded*
*2 large carrots, shredded*
*1 cup mayonnaise*
*1½ tablespoons sugar*
*1 teaspoon celery seed*
*3 tablespoons white vinegar*
*1 teaspoon lemon juice*
*salt and pepper, to taste*

1. In a large bowl, toss cabbage and carrots to combine.
2. In a medium bowl, prepare dressing: whisk and combine mayonnaise, sugar, celery seed, vinegar, lemon juice, salt, and pepper.
3. Pour dressing over cabbage mixture and stir to coat evenly. Cover and refrigerate 1 hour prior to serving.

# Southwestern Fiesta Chicken

MAKES 4 SERVINGS

**CILANTRO LIME RICE**
*1 cup long grain white rice*
*2 cups water*
*1 teaspoon salt*
*juice of 1 lime*
*2–3 tablespoons cilantro,
   chopped*

**FOR THE CHICKEN**
*1-pound boneless, skinless
   chicken breasts, cut into
   two-inch pieces*

*1 packet taco seasoning*
*2 tablespoons olive oil*
*2 cups onion, diced*
*2 cups bell peppers, diced*
*2 cups corn, (fresh or frozen)*
*3–4 garlic cloves, minced*
*14.5 ounce can black beans,
   drained*
*10 ounce can diced tomatoes
   and green chiles, drained*
*1 avocado, diced*

1. In a medium pot, add the rice, water, salt, lime juice, and cilantro. Stir well and bring to a boil, then cover, reduce heat to low, and simmer for 14 minutes. Set aside and keep covered.

2. Season the chicken with half of taco seasoning.

3. In a large skillet heat 1 tablespoon of the olive oil over medium-high heat. Add the chicken in a single layer and cook for 5 minutes, until golden brown, flipping once halfway through. Remove to a plate and set aside.

4. In the same skillet, increase the heat to high, add the remaining olive oil, add onions, bell peppers, corn, and remaining taco seasoning. Cook, stirring occasionally, until veggies are slightly blackened. Decrease heat to low, add garlic, and stir until combined and fragrant, about 30 seconds.

5. Add the drained black beans and tomatoes, rice, and chicken. Stir all to combine.

6. Garnish with extra chopped cilantro and top with diced avocado.

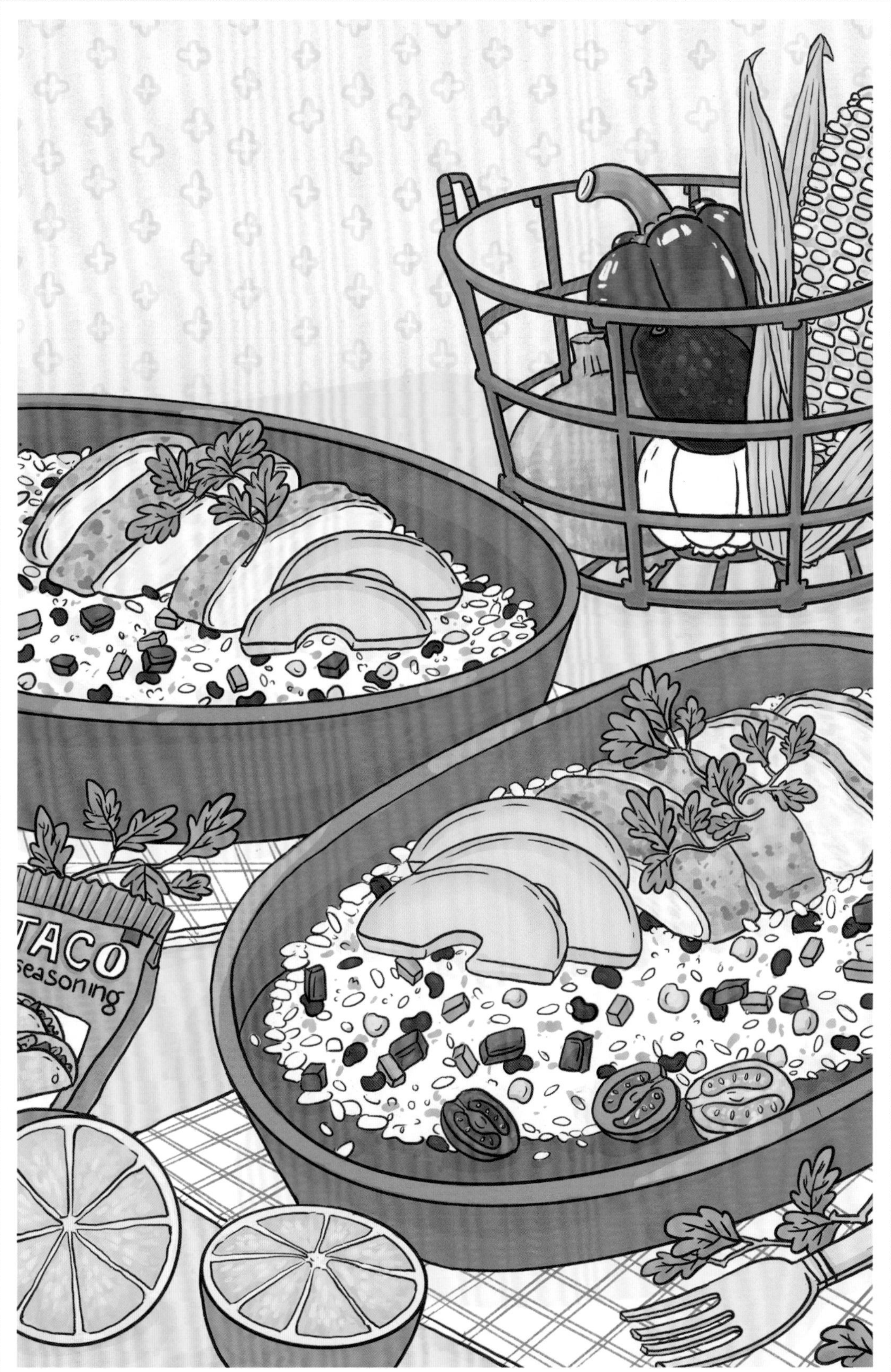
TACO
seasoning

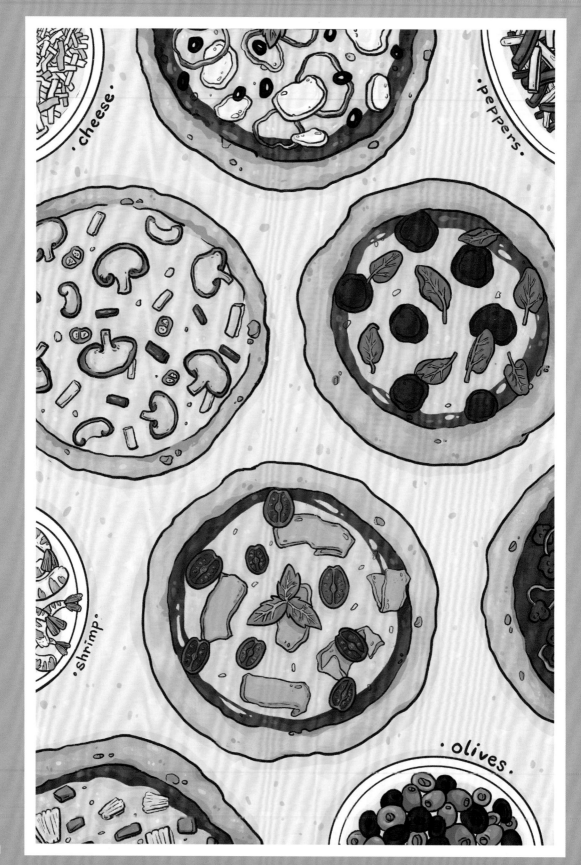

# Mini Pizzas

## MAKES 4 MINI PIZZAS

**TOPPING IDEAS**
*pizza sauce or tomato sauce*
cheese: *Asiago, blue cheese,*
*feta, Mexican cheese,*
*mozzarella, Parmesan,*
*provolone, Romano*
meat: *bacon, chicken, chorizo,*
*ham, Italian sausage,*
*meatballs, pepperoni,*
*prosciutto, shrimp*
other: *artichokes, avocado,*
*fresh basil, garlic, green*
*peppers, jalapeños, olives,*
*onions, mushrooms,*
*pineapple chunks, spinach,*
*squash, tomatoes*

**PIZZA DOUGH**
*1 package active dry yeast*
*1⅓ cups warm water*
*3½ cups all-purpose flour*
*2 teaspoons salt*
*1 teaspoon sugar*
*2 tablespoons extra-virgin*
*olive oil*

1. For Pizza Dough: Oil two medium bowls lightly with olive oil and set aside. Combine yeast and warm water in a small bowl and set aside for 5 minutes.

2. In a large bowl, mix together flour, salt, sugar, and olive oil.

3. Stir in yeast mixture until it combines with flour and begins to form a ball.

4. Knead by hand on a well-floured surface for about 5 minutes and shape into a large dough ball. Divide into two pieces and roll into balls. Place each ball into an oiled bowl, seam side down, and coat tops with a little olive oil. Top each bowl with plastic wrap or a clean, dry towel, place in a warm spot, and let dough rise until doubled in size, about 2 hours.

5. Preheat oven to 400°F and oil a large baking sheet or pizza stone. Turn risen dough onto floured surface and roll out. Use a 4½-inch round cutter to create four pizzas.

6. Arrange mini pizzas on baking sheet and add toppings of your choice. Bake for 13 to 15 minutes, or until cheese is melted and crust is lightly browned.

# Spiral Sandwiches

MAKES 6 SERVINGS

*1 15-inch flour tortilla*
*4 ounces herb-and-garlic spreadable cheese*
*4 slices turkey, staggered and layered*
*6 ounces Swiss cheese, sliced thin*
*1 large tomato, sliced thin*
*18 leaves fresh spinach*

1. Cover one side of tortilla evenly with spreadable cheese.
2. Layer turkey, Swiss cheese, tomato, and spinach on top of spreadable cheese, leaving about 3 inches at one side with spreadable cheese only to assist with roll up.
3. Beginning at side layered with turkey, roll up tortilla, using edge with spreadable cheese to seal. Cut off each end of rolled tortilla to even out and then cut roll into 1-inch slices. Place slices on a serving platter.

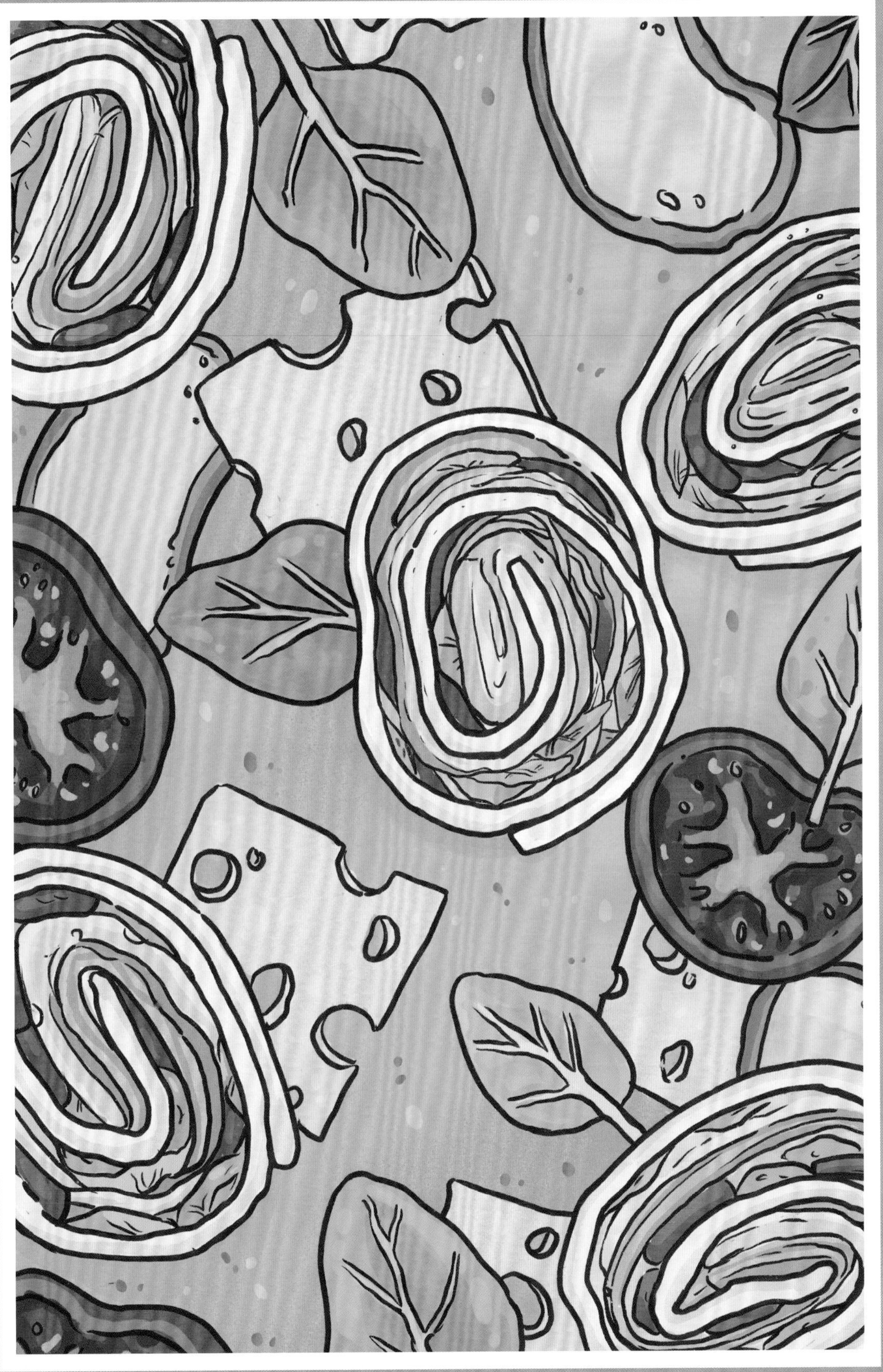

# Caprese Tortellini Pasta Salad

MAKES 6 SERVINGS

*9 ounces cheese tortellini*
*4 ounces fresh mozzarella balls*
*1 pint cherry tomatoes*
*½ cup Italian dressing (recipe below)*
*fresh basil, to taste*

**HOMEMADE ITALIAN DRESSING**
*¼ cup extra virgin olive oil*
*¼ cup white vinegar*
*1 tablespoon Italian seasoning*
*½ tablespoon garlic powder*
*¼ teaspoon salt*

1. Bring a medium pot of water to a boil.
2. Add tortellini and reduce heat to cook according to package directions.
3. Drain tortellini in a colander and run under cold water to halt the cooking process and prevent soggy noodles.
4. Transfer into a medium-large serving bowl along with mozzarella balls, tomatoes, and basil.
5. FOR THE DRESSING: whisk olive oil, white vinegar, italian seasoning, garlic, and salt together and allow to sit.
6. Pour dressing over pasta salad and toss to coat.

# Spaghetti and Meatballs

MAKES 6 SERVINGS

**SPAGHETTI SAUCE**
*3 tablespoons olive oil*
*½ onion, finely chopped*
*4 cloves garlic, minced*
*2 28-ounce cans of crushed
    tomatoes, with juice*
*1 tablespoon sugar*
*salt and pepper to taste*
*2 bay leaves*

**MEATBALLS**
*1 tablespoon olive oil*
*1 small onion, finely chopped*
*1 clove garlic, minced*

*salt and pepper to taste*
*1 pound lean ground beef*
*1 egg, well beaten*
*1 tablespoon Worcestershire
    sauce*
*¼ cup Italian bread crumbs*

**SPAGHETTI**
*1 pound spaghetti*
*water*
*salt*

**TOPPING**
*½ cup freshly grated Parmesan
    cheese*

**SPAGHETTI SAUCE**

1. Heat olive oil in a large saucepan over medium heat. Add onion and garlic. Sauté until onion is soft, about 5 minutes.

2. Add crushed tomatoes with their juice, sugar, salt, pepper, and bay leaves. Bring to a boil and then reduce heat to medium low and simmer until sauce thickens, stirring occasionally, about 1 hour.

**MEATBALLS**

1. While sauce is cooking, preheat oven to 350°F and line a large baking pan with parchment paper.

2. Heat olive oil in a medium frying pan. Cook onion for 3 minutes on medium. Add garlic, salt, and pepper, and cook for 2 minutes longer, being careful not to brown or burn the garlic. Set aside.

3. In a medium bowl, combine beef, egg, Worcestershire sauce, and bread crumbs.

4. Once it has cooled, add onion mixture to meat; mix well.

5. Scoop 2 tablespoons of meat mixture and form into a ball, making 18 meatballs, and arrange in baking pan.

6. Bake for 15 to 20 minutes, until browned and cooked through.
Halfway through baking, stir to ensure even browning.

7. Once meatballs are cooked, gently add to the sauce and continue to simmer, about 10 minutes.

**SPAGHETTI**

1. Cook spaghetti in a large saucepan of boiling salted water until tender but still firm to bite.

2. Drain spaghetti in a colander and transfer to serving bowls. Spoon sauce with meatballs over pasta and sprinkle with Parmesan cheese.

# Roasted Vegetables

MAKES 12 SERVINGS

*1 pound white potatoes*
*1 pound Brussels sprouts*
*1 medium onion*
*½ pound broccoli florets*
*3 large carrots*
*½ pound cauliflower florets*
*1 large, sweet potato*
*3 garlic cloves, minced*
*¼ cup olive oil*
*½ teaspoon kosher salt*
*¼ teaspoon pepper*

1. Preheat oven to 375°F place a large, rimmed baking sheet on center rack to heat up along with the oven.
2. Rinse and cut vegetables into uniform pieces, each about 1 square inch. Place all vegetables and garlic in a large bowl and drizzle with olive oil. Toss to coat and season with salt and pepper.
3. Pour prepared vegetables onto the hot pan and spread into an even layer. Bake for 75 to 90 minutes, tossing 35 minutes into cooking so the vegetables evenly brown. Remove from oven when vegetables are brown and crispy and serve immediately.

# Crispy Baked Black Bean and Sweet Potato Tacos

### MAKES 8 TACOS

*1 medium sweet potato, peeled
  and diced*
*1 tablespoon olive oil*
*1 cup refried black beans*
*8 medium corn tortillas*
*1 cup cheddar cheese, grated*

TOPPINGS
*guacamole (see below)*
*shredded cheese*
*sour cream*
*salsa*

1. In a steamer basket over 1 inch of simmering water, steam sweet potato until it is tender when stuck with a fork, approximately 15 to 20 minutes. Mash thoroughly with a fork.

2. Preheat oven to 400°F. Line a large baking sheet with parchment paper and brush with olive oil.

3. Spread 1 tablespoon refried beans on half of a tortilla; top with 1 tablespoon sweet potato and a tablespoon of cheese.

4. Fold tortilla in half, brush top with olive oil, and place on baking sheet. Repeat with other tortillas and rest of ingredients. Bake for 10 minutes, flipping once.

5. Let tacos cool for a few minutes and top with Guacamole.

## Guacamole

*3 avocados, peeled, pitted,
  and mashed*
*1 lime, juiced*
*½ cup onion, diced*
*3 tablespoons fresh cilantro, chopped*
*3 tomatoes, diced*
*1 teaspoon garlic, minced*

*Salt to taste*

In a medium bowl, mash together avocados and lime juice. Add onion, cilantro, tomatoes, garlic, and salt and mix well.

# Pizza Stuffed Crescent Rolls

MAKES 8 SERVINGS

*8 ounces crescent rolls*
*½ cup pepperoni*
*4 mozzarella cheese sticks, cut in half*
*2 tablespoons unsalted butter, melted*
*¼ teaspoon Italian seasoning*
*½ teaspoon garlic salt*
*2 tablespoons parmesan cheese, grated*
*1 cup marinara sauce*

1. Preheat oven to 375°F.
2. Line a baking sheet with parchment paper or a silicone mat and separate rolls into triangles.
3. Place pepperoni on the widest part of the triangle. Place a piece of mozzarella on top. Roll the wide end of the dough to the thin end and tuck in the ends to seal the roll. Repeat with all rolls.
4. Brush the rolls with melted butter and sprinkle Italian seasoning and garlic salt on top of rolls.
5. Bake 10 to 14 minutes or until rolls are golden brown.
6. Serve warm with marinara sauce for dipping.

# Roasted Mini Peppers

MAKES 6 SERVINGS

*2 (16 ounces packages) of sweet mini peppers, rinsed and sliced in*
*    half lengthwise*
*2 tablespoons of olive oil*
*3 garlic cloves, minced*
*kosher salt and pepper to taste*
*fresh basil, optional for garnish*
*fresh thyme, optional for garnish*

1. Preheat oven to 425°F.
2. In a medium bowl toss peppers with olive oil, garlic, salt, and pepper.
3. Spread peppers on sheet pan and bake in the oven for 20 minutes, serve immediately.

# Fish Sticks

MAKES 4 SERVINGS

*2 white fish fillets tilapia, cod, or catfish*
*½ teaspoon salt*
*¼ teaspoon black pepper*
*1 large egg*
*2 tablespoons half and half*
*¼ cup all-purpose flour*
*⅓ cup plain breadcrumbs*
*¼ teaspoon garlic powder*
*¼ teaspoon Italian seasoning*
*½ cup vegetable oil for frying in pan*

1. Preheat oven to 375°F, and line a baking sheet with parchment paper.

2. Slice fillets into ¾" wide pieces.

3. In a shallow dish, whisk egg and half and half; in another dish, place flour; in the last dish, combine breadcrumbs with garlic powder and Italian seasoning.

4. Season fish pieces with salt and pepper.

5. Dip each fish stick in flour first, then egg mixture, then finally in breadcrumbs. Coat evenly, shake of excess. Repeat with all fish pieces. Set them on a plate next to stove. Prepare another plate with a paper towel.

6. Bake fish sticks for 15 to 18 minutes.

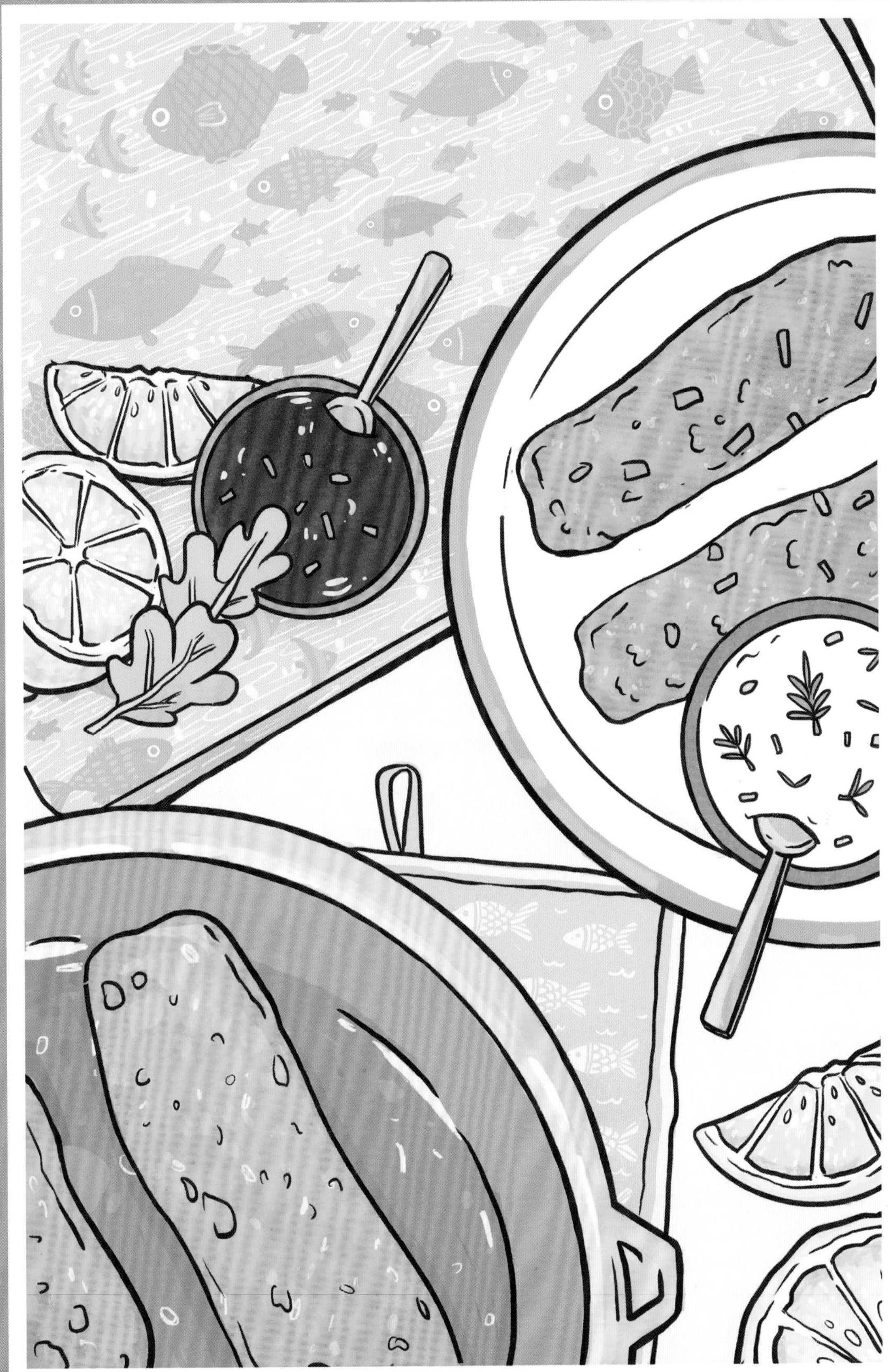

# Watermelon Cucumber Salad

MAKES 6 SERVINGS

*8 cups seedless watermelon, cubed*
*2 mini cucumbers, sliced*
*2 ounces feta cheese, crumbled*
*zest of ½ a lemon*
*4 basil leaves*
*sea salt, for garnish*

1. On a large platter arrange the watermelon, cucumbers, and sprinkle with feta, lemon zest, and sea salt.
2. Serve immediately

# Taco Cups

MAKES 6 SERVINGS

*1 pound of ground beef or turkey, browned and drained*
*15 ounce can refried beans*
*15 ounce can diced tomatoes, drained*
*¾ cup sharp cheddar cheese, shredded*
*1 teaspoon garlic powder*
*1 teaspoon onion powder*
*1 teaspoon cumin or chili powder*
*½ teaspoon salt*
*¼ teaspoon pepper*
*¼ teaspoon crushed red pepper flakes*
*10 6-inch gluten-free tortillas*

1. Preheat the oven to 375°F and spray a muffin tin with non-stick cooking spray.

2. In a medium skillet, brown meat, drain and return to pan. Add garlic powder, onion powder, cumin, salt, pepper, and red pepper flakes, diced tomatoes, and refried beans.

3. Fold tortillas into muffin tins. Divide meat mixture evenly between tortilla cups. Top with cheese.

4. Bake 8 to 10 minutes or until shells are crispy and browned.

# Chicken Pot Pie

MAKES 8 SERVINGS

4 tablespoons unsalted butter
1 pound boneless skinless
   chicken breast, cut into
   2-inch pieces
1 cup carrots, sliced
½ cup celery, sliced
½ cup yellow onion, chopped
1¼ teaspoons salt
½ teaspoon garlic powder
½ teaspoon dried thyme leaves

¼ teaspoon ground black
   pepper
¼ cup all-purpose flour
½ cup heavy cream
1 cup chicken broth
½ cup peas, frozen
2 tablespoons minced fresh
   flat-leaf parsley
2 unbaked pie crusts

1. Preheat oven to 425°F.
2. In a large skillet, over medium heat add the butter. Once the butter is melted, add the chicken, carrots, celery, onion, salt, garlic powder, thyme leaves, and pepper. Cook for 8 to 10 minutes, until the chicken is cooked through, stirring often.
3. Add the flour. Stir well, until no dry flour remains. Slowly stir in the cream, then the chicken broth. Cook until bubbling and thick, stirring often, 3 to 4 minutes.
4. Remove from the heat. Stir in the peas and flat leaf parsley. Let this cool for 15 to 30 minutes before filling the pie.
5. Fit one pie crust into a 9-inch pie plate. Spoon the cooled filling into the pie crust. Top with the second pie crust. Seal the edges of the pie crust together. Cut 3 to 4 slits in the top crust to allow steam to escape.
6. Place the filled pie plate on a baking sheet. Bake for 30 minutes on the bottom rack of the oven.
7. Cool for 15 to 30 minutes before slicing and serving.

# Mini Meatloaf's

## MAKES 8 MEATLOAFS

*1 pound ground beef*
*½ pound ground pork*
*¾ cup breadcrumbs*
*2 large eggs*
*¾ cup whole milk*
*2 teaspoons sea salt*
*1 teaspoon Italian seasoning*
*¼ teaspoon black pepper, ground*
*1 teaspoon garlic powder*
*1 teaspoon onion powder*
*¼ cup ketchup*
*2 tablespoon brown sugar*
*2 teaspoons Worcestershire sauce*
*1 teaspoon water*
*¾ pound broccoli, florets*
*¾ baby potatoes, halved*
*2 tablespoons olive oil*

1.  Preheat oven to 350°F and grease a
    baking sheet and set aside.

2.  In a large bowl, mix the ground beef, pork,
    and breadcrumbs until fully combined.

3.  In a medium bowl, whisk the eggs, milk,
    1¼ teaspoon salt, Italian seasoning,
    pepper, garlic powder, and onion powder.

4.  In a small bowl, whisk the eggs together
    with 3 tablespoons of ketchup and add
    mixture into the meat and mix until fully
    combined.

5. In a small bowl mix together the remaining 1 tablespoon of ketchup, brown sugar, Worcestershire sauce and water until fully combined.

6. Place the broccoli and potatoes on the baking sheet and drizzle with olive oil and the remaining ¾ teaspoon of salt. Toss to coat evenly and spread evenly on baking pan.

7. Divide the meat into eight small loafs approx. 4″ x 3″ oval shaped and spread-out loaves between the broccoli and potatoes.

8. Brush the brown sugar sauce over the top of each mini meatloaf.

9. Bake in the oven for 30 minutes. Remove from oven and allow to cool slightly before serving with the broccoli and potatoes.

# Quick and Easy Pasta

MAKES 4 SERVINGS

*3 cups pasta of your choice*
*water to boil pasta*
*salt to taste*
*2 teaspoons olive oil*
*2 large tomatoes, chopped*
*1 teaspoon paprika*
*¼ teaspoon cayenne powder*
*½ teaspoon dried oregano*
*½ teaspoon dried basil*
*1 cup cheddar cheese, shredded*
*1 cup mozzarella cheese, shredded*
*black pepper, to taste*
*pinch of red pepper, crushed (optional)*

1.  Bring a large pot of salted water to a boil. Add pasta and cook according to the instructions on the package.

2.  While pasta cooks, in a large skillet, warm olive oil and add chopped tomatoes. Mix well, and add salt, paprika, cayenne pepper, oregano, and basil. Mix well and cook until tomatoes are soft.

3.  Once pasta is cooked, with a slotted spoon, remove pasta from the pot and add to the tomato mixture. Reserve the pasta water, to use it later.

4.  Mix the pasta with tomato mixture. Add the cheddar and mozzarella cheeses and mix well. Add 2-3 tablespoons of reserved pasta water into the tomato-pasta mixture. If your Pasta looks dry, you can add more pasta water.

5.  Cook for 3 to 4 minutes or until cheese is melted. Season with black pepper and if using, crushed red pepper. Serve hot.

POTATOES

# Shepherd's Pie

MAKES 6 SERVINGS

MEAT FILLING
2 tablespoons olive oil
1 cup yellow onion, chopped
1 pound lean ground beef or
  ground lamb
2 teaspoons dried parsley
1 teaspoon dried rosemary
1 teaspoon dried thyme
½ teaspoon salt
½ teaspoon ground black
  pepper
1 tablespoon Worcestershire
  sauce
2 cloves garlic, minced
1 tablespoon all-purpose flour
2 tablespoons tomato paste

1 cup beef broth
1 cup frozen peas
  and carrots
½ cup frozen corn kernels

POTATO TOPPING
1½–2 pounds russet potatoes,
  peeled and cut into 1-inch
  cubes
8 tablespoons unsalted butter
⅓ cup half-and-half
½ teaspoon garlic powder
½ teaspoon salt
¼ teaspoon ground
  black pepper
¼ cup Parmesan cheese

**MEAT FILLING**

1. In a medium frying pan, heat olive oil over medium-high heat for 2 minutes. Sauté onion for 5 minutes.

2. Put ground beef (or ground lamb) into frying pan and break it apart with a wooden spoon. Add parsley, rosemary, thyme, salt, and pepper and mix well. Cook until meat is browned, approximately 6 to 8 minutes.

3. Stir in Worcestershire sauce and garlic and cook for 1 minute.

4. Add flour and tomato paste, mixing until no clumps of tomato paste remain.

5. Pour in broth and add peas, carrots, and corn. Bring liquid to a boil and then reduce heat. Simmer for 5 minutes, stirring occasionally.

6. Set meat mixture aside. Preheat oven to 400°F.

**POTATO TOPPING**

1. Place potatoes in a large saucepan and fully cover them with water. Bring water to a boil and then reduce to a simmer. Cook for 10 to 15 minutes, until potatoes are tender when a fork is inserted.

2. Drain potatoes in a colander and return them to saucepan.

3. Add butter, half-and-half, garlic powder, salt, and pepper. Mash potatoes until all ingredients are mixed together.

4. Stir in Parmesan cheese until well combined; potatoes should be smooth.

**ASSEMBLY**

1. Preheat oven to 350°F.

2. Pour meat mixture into a 9 × 9 (or 7 × 11)-inch baking dish, spreading it into an even layer.

3. Spoon an even layer of mashed potatoes on top of meat.

4. Bake uncovered for 25 to 30 minutes.

# Rosemary Roasted Potatoes

MAKES 4 SERVINGS

*1½ pounds baby red potatoes, halved*
*3 teaspoons kosher salt*
*2 tablespoons extra-virgin olive oil*
*2 teaspoons garlic powder*
*2 tablespoons fresh rosemary leaves, minced*

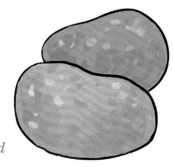

1. Preheat the oven to 475°F.

2. Fill a large pot with water and 1½ teaspoons of the salt. Bring to a boil over high heat. Add the potatoes and cook until just tender, about 10 minutes. Drain the potatoes in a colander and put aside to cool and dry.

3. In a large bowl, combine the potatoes, olive oil, garlic powder, rosemary, and the remaining 1½ teaspoons salt. Toss to coat well and serve.

# Chicken Fingers and Fries

MAKES 4 SERVINGS

**CHICKEN FINGERS**

*1 cup whole wheat flour*

*2 teaspoon salt, divided*

*2 cups Panko breadcrumbs*

*3 eggs*

*¼ cup water*

*1 pound chicken tenders*

**FRIES**

*1 teaspoon garlic powder*

*½ teaspoon dried thyme*

*¼ teaspoon dried oregano*

*¾ teaspoon sea salt*

*¼ teaspoon freshly ground black pepper*

*2 pounds russet potatoes*

*2 tablespoon olive oil*

## CHICKEN FINGERS

1. Preheat oven to 425°F.

2. Place an oven-safe cooling rack on a rimmed baking sheet. Lightly spray with nonstick spray.

3. In a large resealable bag add flour and one teaspoon of salt. In a second bag Panko breadcrumbs.

4. Whisk eggs and water together with remaining teaspoon of salt in a shallow dish.

5. Place chicken into flour bag, tossing to coat. Shake off excess. Dip into egg wash, and then finally into bag with breadcrumbs, using your hands to help breadcrumbs coat chicken strips.

6. Place breaded chicken tenders on prepared baking sheet.

7. Bake for 10 to 13 minutes, or until chicken reaches an internal temperature of 165°F.

## FRIES

1. Preheat oven to 425°F.

2. In a small bowl, stir to combine garlic powder, thyme, oregano, salt, and pepper.

3. Scrub potato skins with a stiff brush. If you don't like skin, peel it off with a vegetable peeler.

4. Cut potatoes into wedges. First carefully cut potato in half and then keep cutting each piece in half until each potato is cut into sixteen pieces.

5. Toss potatoes with oil, sprinkle with seasoning, and then spread them out in a single layer on a baking sheet. Make sure potato wedges aren't touching one another, or they won't brown.

6. Bake for about 20 minutes, until fries are turning golden brown on edges.

7. Flip potatoes over and bake for another 5 to 10 minutes, until golden brown all over.

8. Season with extra salt if desired.

# Creamy Potato Soup

MAKES 6 SERVINGS

*6 slices bacon, uncooked*
*4 tablespoons unsalted butter*
*2 large leeks, trimmed and chopped*
*2 garlic cloves, minced*
*¼ cup all-purpose flour*
*2 pounds russet potatoes, peeled and cut into 1-inch cubes*
*1 quart chicken stock*
*1 cup milk*
*1 cup heavy cream*
*2 teaspoons kosher salt*
*½ teaspoon pepper*
*½ cup sharp white cheddar cheese, grated*
*2 green onions, thinly sliced*

1. In a large pot cook the bacon until bacon crisps, 5 to 7 minutes. Transfer the bacon to a paper toweled lined plate, reserving the fat in the pot.

2. Add the butter to pan with the bacon fat and cook until melted. Stir in the leeks and the garlic and cook until leeks are softened, about 4 minutes. Sprinkle the flour over the mixture and stir until well combined.

3. Add the potatoes, chicken stock, milk, and heavy cream. Bring to a boil over high heat, then reduce the heat to a simmer. Cover and cook for 10 minutes or until the potatoes are very soft.

4. Transfer half the liquid to a blender, let cool briefly, and blend until smooth. Return the blended soup to the pot. Use an immersion blender in a large bowl to blend the remaining unblended liquid and return to pot. Stir the bacon, salt, pepper, and cheese into the pot mix until cheese melts.

5. Ladle the soup into bowls and top with green onions, pepper, and cheese prior to serving.

# Cheeseburger Tater Tot Casserole

### MAKES 8 SERVINGS

*1 pound lean ground beef*
*⅓ cup diced yellow onion*
*⅔ cup ketchup*
*2 tablespoons yellow mustard*
*2 tablespoons relish*
*2 tablespoons butter*
*2 tablespoons all-purpose flour*
*1½ cups milk*
*¼ teaspoon salt*

*¼ teaspoon black pepper*
*2 cups shredded cheddar*
*    cheese, divided*
*32-ounce bag Tater Tot*
*    potatoes*

1.  Preheat oven to 350°F. Spray a casserole dish with nonstick cooking spray.

2.  In a large skillet over medium heat, cook beef and onion stirring occasionally, until beef is brown; drain.

3.  Stir in ketchup, mustard and relish. Add salt and pepper to taste. Spoon mixture into prepared casserole dish and smooth into an even layer.

4.  In a medium saucepan over medium heat, melt butter completely. Slowly whisk in the flour until smooth.

5.  Slowly whisk in the milk, stirring until well combined; about 5 minutes. Stir in salt and pepper. Remove the pan from heat and whisk in 1 1/2 cups of cheese until it is completely melted, and the sauce is smooth.

6.  Evenly pour the sauce over the meat mixture. Arrange the frozen Tater Tots potatoes in an even layer over the cheese sauce.

7.  Bake in preheated oven for 35 minutes. Remove from oven and sprinkle remaining cheese onto the tots. Return to the oven for an additional 5 minutes, or until the cheese is melted.

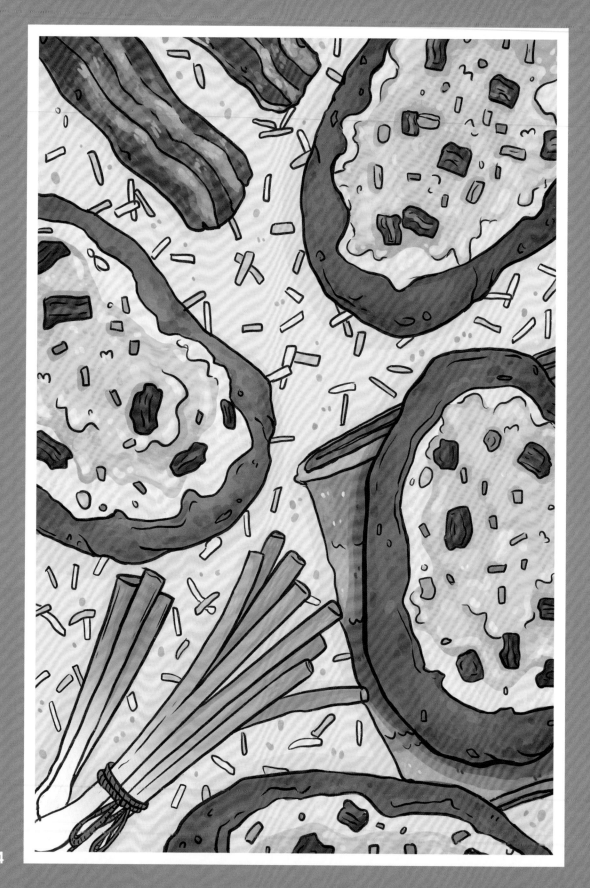

# Cheddar and Bacon Twice-Baked Potatoes

MAKES 6 SERVINGS

8 slices bacon, cooked and
    crumbled
6 large russet potatoes,
    scrubbed and dried
olive oil
salt

4 green onions, sliced
1 cup cheddar cheese, grated
½ cup sour cream
6 tablespoons unsalted butter
freshly ground black pepper

1. Preheat oven to 350°F. Place potatoes on a baking sheet, prick with a fork, drizzle lightly with olive oil, and sprinkle with salt. Bake until cooked through, about 1 hour. Potato skins will be crisp and insides tender when poked with a fork. Let cool.

2. With a paring knife, cut an oval shape from top of each potato and discard top. Use a spoon to scoop out inside of potato and place into a medium bowl. An empty potato skin will remain.

3. Put cheese and green onions into bowl with potato, reserving a sprinkle of each for topping.

4. Add crumbled bacon, sour cream, butter, salt, and pepper to bowl and mix well.

5. Scoop equal portions of potato filling into skins and sprinkle tops with reserved cheese and green onion.

6. Return each potato to baking sheet and bake until golden and heated through, about 25 minutes.

# Potato-Bacon Hash

## MAKES 6 SERVINGS

*6 thick-cut bacon slices*
*1½ pounds russet potatoes, peeled and cut into ½ inch pieces*
*1 cup yellow onion, chopped*
*1 cup red bell pepper, chopped*
*1 teaspoon garlic, chopped*
*1 teaspoon kosher salt*
*½ teaspoon black pepper*
*4 cups baby spinach*

1. In a large skillet, over medium heat cook bacon until crispy, 10 to 12 minutes, Transfer to a plate lined with paper towels, reserving fat in skillet.

2. Add potatoes, onion, and bell pepper to skillet, cover and cook over medium heat until potatoes soften, about 5 minutes. Uncover and cook, without stirring until potatoes are just browned. Stir in garlic, salt, and pepper. Continue to cook 12 minutes, gently stirring every three minutes or until potatoes have browned.

3. Add bacon and spinach to the skillet and remove from heat. Stir until spinach begins to wilt.

# Vegan Roasted Sweet Potato Salad

MAKES 8-10 SERVINGS

*3 sweet potatoes, cut into 2-inch cubes*
*2 tablespoons olive oil*
*2 tablespoons taco seasoning*
*2 bunches kale, stems removed and torn into 2-inch pieces*
*½ cup cilantro leaves*
*3 green onions, thinly sliced*
*1 can black beans, rinsed and drained*
*1 avocado, sliced*

**VEGAN CILANTRO-CASHEW DRESSING**
*½ cup cilantro*
*3 garlic cloves*
*2 tablespoons lime juice*
*½ teaspoon sea salt*
*3 tablespoons extra virgin olive oil*
*½ cup raw cashews*
*¾ cup water*
*½ jalapeno, seeded, (optional)*
*½ avocado*

1. Preheat oven to 400°F.
2. In a large bowl, toss sweet potatoes, with olive oil and taco seasoning.
3. Arrange potatoes on a baking sheet and cook in oven on middle rack for 30 minutes, flipping over potatoes halfway through.
4. In a blender combine cilantro, garlic, lime juice, sea salt, olive oil, cashews, water, jalapeno (if using), and avocado.
5. In medium bowl, add cooked potatoes and pour in dressing and mix.

# Scalloped Potatoes

## MAKES 8-10 SERVINGS

*4 pounds white potatoes, sliced*
*2 teaspoons kosher salt*
*1 teaspoon ground black pepper*
*1 cup parmesan cheese, shredded*
*1 cup cheddar cheese, shredded*
*½ cup heavy whipping cream*
*chives, fresh and chopped for garnish*

1. Preheat oven to 400°F. Spray a 13 x 9 baking dish with non-stick spray.

2. Arrange ⅓ of sliced potatoes in bottom of pan. Sprinkle potatoes with ½ teaspoon salt, ¼ teaspoon pepper, and ¼ cup of each Parmesan and cheddar cheese. Repeat layers twice. Drizzle cream onto potatoes and top with remaining salt, pepper, and cheeses.

3. Bake until potatoes are tender, and top is golden brown, about 1 hour. Let stand for 5 minutes prior to serving. Garnish with chives, if desired.

# Potato Casserole

MAKES 8 SERVINGS

*30 ounces frozen hash browns, defrosted*
*2 cups sour cream*
*one 10.5 ounce can cream of chicken soup*
*10 tablespoons butter, melted*
*1 teaspoon salt*
*¼ teaspoon freshly ground*
*black pepper*
*1 teaspoon dried minced onion*
*2 cups shredded cheddar cheese*
*2 cups cornflakes cereal*

1. Allow potatoes to thaw in fridge overnight or spread them on a baking sheet and warm them in oven at 200°F for about 20 minutes, until thawed.

2. Preheat oven to 350°F.

3. Combine sour cream, cream of chicken soup, 6 tablespoons melted butter, salt, pepper, and dried onion in a bowl. Mix well.

4. Add potatoes and shredded cheese and stir to combine. Spoon mixture into a single layer in a 9 × 13-inch pan.

5. Put cornflakes in a large resealable bag and crush gently with your hands or a rolling pin. Pour in a bowl.

6. Add remaining 4 tablespoons melted butter to crushed cornflakes and combine well. Sprinkle mixture over potatoes.

7. Bake uncovered at 350°F for 40 to 50 minutes.

# Potato Salad

MAKES 8 SERVINGS

*6–8 medium Yukon Gold potatoes, peeled (about 2 pounds)*
*¼ cup red onion, chopped*
*3 stalks celery, chopped*
*3 eggs, hard boiled, chopped*
*1 cup mayonnaise*
*2 teaspoons yellow mustard*
*¼ cup sweet relish*
*1 teaspoon salt*
*½ teaspoon black pepper*
*½ teaspoon paprika*

1. Add potatoes to a large pot, cover with water (1 to 2 inches above potatoes), and cook until fork-tender.
2. Remove potatoes from pot, let cool for 10 minutes, and cut into 2-inch cubes.
3. In a large bowl, add chopped potatoes, onion, celery, and eggs.
4. In a small bowl, combine mayonnaise, mustard, relish, salt, pepper, and paprika and whisk until well combined.
5. Add dressing to potatoes and stir gently to combine.
6. Cover and store in refrigerator until ready to serve.

# Chocolate Cake with Vanilla frosting

SERVES 12-16

### CAKE

*3/4 cup Dutch process cocoa
    powder (the dutch process
    makes a difference!)*
*1¼ cups all-purpose flour*
*½ teaspoon baking soda*
*¼ teaspoon salt*
*8 ounces semisweet chocolate,
    cut into thin small pieces*
*12 tablespoons butter*
*4 eggs*
*1½ cups sugar*
*1½ teaspoons vanilla extract*
*1 cup buttermilk*

### FROSTING

*2 sticks softened butter
    (unsalted)*
*¼ teaspoon salt*
*1 tablespoon vanilla extract*
*3 ½ cups confectioners' sugar,
    sifted*
*4 tablespoons milk (I used 1%)*

1. Pre-heat your oven to 325°F.
2. In a small bowl, combine 8 ounces semisweet chocolate with butter. Microwave at 50% power for about 2 minutes, or until the chocolate is melted. Stir well until the butter and chocolate are melted together and smooth.
3. While the chocolate/butter combo is melting in the microwave, grease the bottom and sides of 2 8-inch cake pans.
4. In a medium bowl, sift together the dry ingredients: flour, baking soda, salt, and cocoa powder.
5. In a separate medium bowl, use a whisk to combine sugar, vanilla, and eggs. Stir in buttermilk until smooth.
6. In a large bowl combine chocolate/butter combo with the egg mixture.

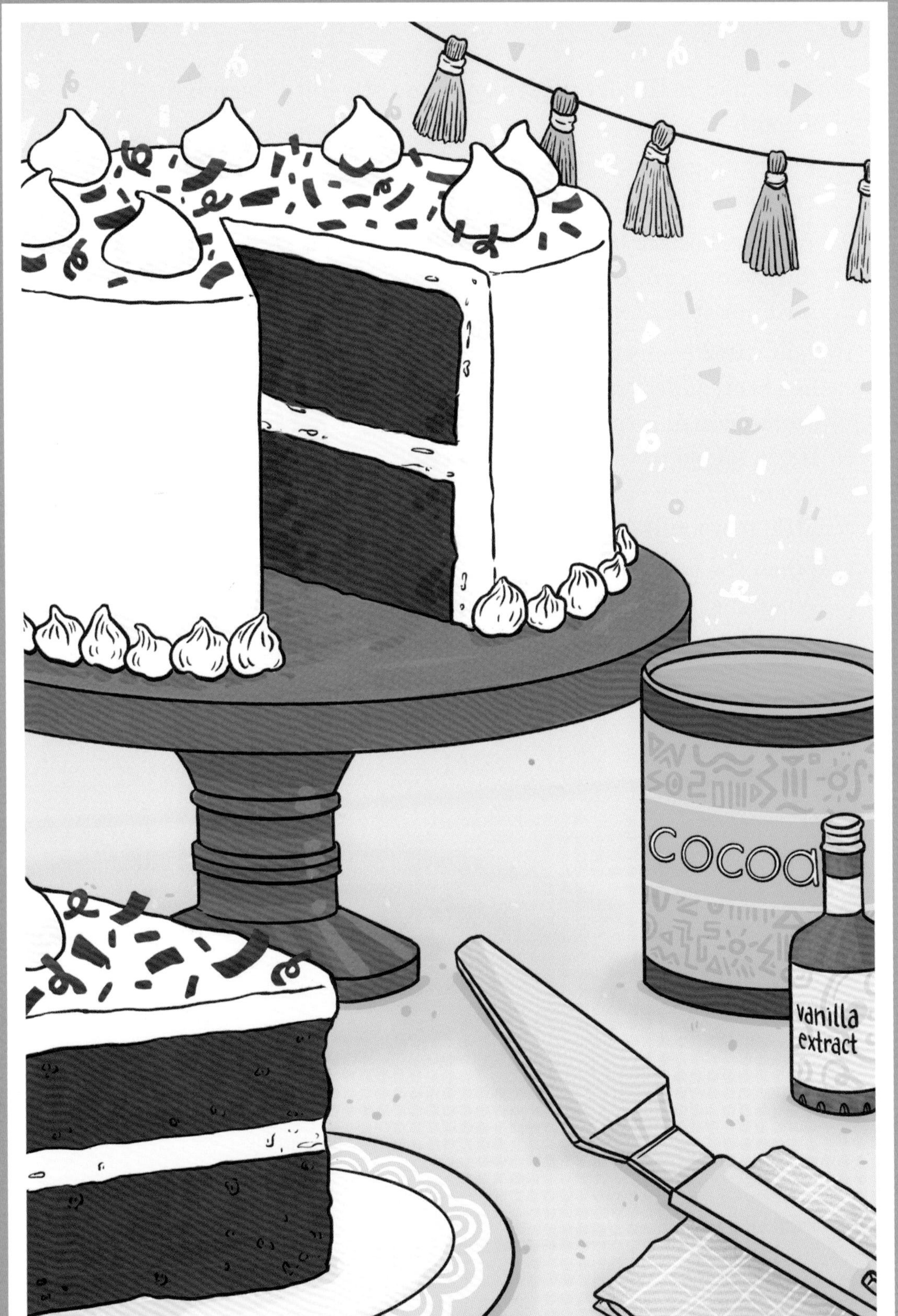
COCOA
vanilla extract

7. Next, add in the dry ingredients and stir until the mixture is smooth.

8. Pour into greased pans and bake for about 40 minutes, or until a toothpick inserted in the middle of the cake comes out clean.

9. While cakes are baking, prepare the frosting. Place the butter in the mixer bowl. Using the paddle attachment, mix the butter on medium speed until it's light and fluffy. Mix in salt and vanilla.

10. Add sifted confectioners' sugar one cup at a time, until all sugar has been added, mixing well in between each cup. Add milk one tablespoon at a time until you've reached your desired consistency. If you added too much milk, just add a little more confectioners' sugar. If you've added too much confectioners' sugar, just add a little more milk.

11. When the cake is done baking, allow it to cool for at least an hour. When it's cool to touch, frost the top of one cake, place the second cake on top and frost the top and sides all around.

# Key Lime Pie

SERVES 6-8

*1½ cups graham cracker crumbs*
*¼ cup sugar*
*½ teaspoon cinnamon*
*½ cup butter, melted*
*1 14 ounces can sweetened condensed milk*
*3 egg yolks*
*½ cup fresh squeezed lime juice*
*whipped cream for serving*
*lime slices for garnish*

1. Preheat oven to 350°F and grease a 9-inch pie pan.
2. In a medium bowl, combine graham cracker crumbs, sugar and cinnamon and mix until well combined.
3. Add melted butter and stir until the mixture resembles wet sand.
4. Press into a 9-inch pie pan and bake 6 to 8 minutes at 350°F.
5. Remove from oven and cool.
6. In a large bowl, combine sweetened condensed milk and egg yolks whisk until smooth.
7. Add lime juice and whisk until smooth.
8. Pour filling into the pie crust and bake at 350°F for 10 minutes.
9. Cool on wire rack for 1 hour.
10. Chill pie in the refrigerator 4 hours or overnight.
11. Top with whipped cream and garnish with lime slices.

# No Bake Cookies and Cream Bars

MAKES 9 SERVINGS

*16 ounce package of Oreo cookies*
*5 cups large marshmallows*
*4 tablespoons butter*

1. Line a 8 x 8 inch baking pan with foil and set aside.
2. In a food processor pulse Oreos until ground.
3. Melt marshmallows and butter in microwave until puffed, about 1½ to 2 minutes.
4. Pour ground Oreos into marshmallows stirring to combine then transfer to the prepared baking pan.
5. Let set up for 10 minutes. Remove bars out of pan with edges of foil and cut into equal squares.

# Cherry Hand Pies

MAKES 12–14 PIES

*1 14 ounces pie crust or homemade*
*21 ounce can cherry pie filling*
*1 egg*
*1 tablespoon water*

1. Preheat oven to 425°F and line baking sheet with parchment paper.
2. Unroll pie crust use a biscuit cutter to cut 4″ circles. Ball up and roll out remaining dough to cut additional circles.
3. Place each dough circle on parchment paper in pan and top with 1 tablespoon of cherry filling.
4. Fold the dough circle in half crimping the edges with a fork to seal.
5. In a small bowl whisk together egg and water.
6. Brush each hand pie with egg wash until completely coated.
7. Sprinkle with sugar and poke a fork in the center of hand pie to vent.
8. Bake for 15 minutes until golden brown.
9. Remove from oven and allow to cool slightly prior to serving.

# Banana Pudding

MAKES 10 SERVINGS

*2 cups cold milk*
*1 teaspoon vanilla extract*
*2 (3.4 ounces) instant vanilla pudding packages*
*14 ounces sweetened condensed milk*
*2 cups heavy whipping cream*
*11 ounces vanilla wafers*
*4 fresh bananas*
*3 tablespoons powdered sugar*

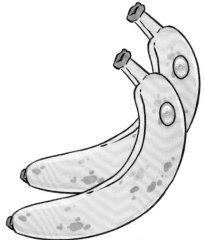

1. In a large bowl, beat the cold milk with the vanilla extract and vanilla pudding until it thickens. Pour in the condensed milk and beat to combine.

2. In a separate bowl, beat the heavy whipping cream until smooth peaks form. Add about ⅔ of the whipped cream into the pudding and gently fold in with a spatula.

3. Add the powdered sugar into the remaining ⅓ whipped cream and fold with a spatula to combine. Refrigerate until needed.

4. Add about ¼ of the vanilla wafers into the bottom of a trifle bowl and about ¼ of the bananas.

5. Spread ¼ of the pudding over the bananas/wafers. Repeat layering until you have four layers.

6. Top it off with the reserved whipped cream and decorate top as as you wish. Cover and refrigerate 2 hours prior to serving.

# Chocolate-Covered Bananas

## MAKES 6 SERVINGS

*3 bananas*
*1 cup chocolate chips*

OPTIONAL TOPPINGS
*nuts*
*pumpkin seeds*
*shredded coconut*
*almond butter or peanut butter*
*dried cranberries*
*sprinkles*

1. Peel bananas, slice in half, and insert a food-safe ice pop stick into each cut end.

2. Lay bananas on a piece of parchment paper or wax paper and freeze for at least 2 hours.

3. Melt chocolate in a double boiler, or in microwave for 20 seconds at a time. Check to make sure chocolate is melted; do not overcook.

4. Dip each frozen banana into melted chocolate and then twirl to remove excess chocolate.

5. Sprinkle toppings on banana while chocolate is still wet. Place on parchment paper to allow chocolate to fully harden.

# Cranberry-Orange Butter Cookies

## MAKES 60 COOKIES

1½ cups unsalted butter
1¼ cups unsifted powdered sugar
2 teaspoons vanilla extract
3 cups all-purpose flour
¼ teaspoon plus ⅛ teaspoon baking powder
¼ teaspoon salt
¾ cups dried cranberries, chopped
1½ tablespoons orange zest
1 cup sugar for dusting

1. Beat butter with a standard mixer fitted with paddle attachment on medium speed until creamy. Gradually add powdered sugar, beating until smooth. Beat in vanilla extract.

2. In a medium bowl, stir together the flour, baking powder, and salt. Gradually add this mixture to the butter mixture, beating on low speed until well combined, about a minute. Beat in cranberries and orange zest until just combined, about 30 seconds.

3. Divide dough in half. Shape each half into a rectangle log about 9 inches long x 2 inches wide x 2 inches tall. Wrap in plastic wrap and chill at least two hours or overnight in the refrigerator.

4. Preheat oven to 350°F. Place sugar in a shallow dish. Unwrap dough and press sugar onto dough logs.

5. Cut dough into ¼ inch thick slices. Arrange slices 1 inch apart on two parchment lined baking sheets.

6. Working in batches, if necessary, bake cookies 10 to 12 minutes or until lightly browned. Cook on baking sheets five minutes. Transfer cookies to wire racks to cool completely.

# No Bake Haystack Cookies

MAKES 24 COOKIES

*10 ounces white chocolate*
*11 ounces butterscotch chips*
*1 cup creamy peanut butter*
*15 ounces crunchy chow mein noodles*

1. Line a baking sheet with parchment paper and set aside.
2. In a medium pot on low, melt the white chocolate and butterscotch chips. Stir constantly and remove from heat once melted.
3. Fold in the peanut butter and chow mein noodles.
4. Use a cookie scoop to scoop out even helpings and place one inch apart on prepared baking sheet. Once tray is full place in the refrigerator for 15 to 20 minutes for your haystacks to chill.

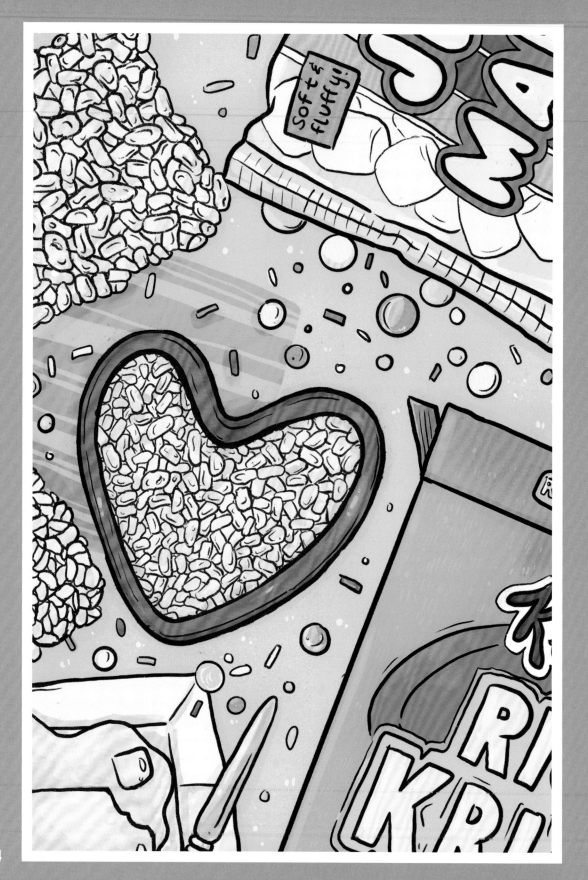

# Rice Crispy Hearts

### MAKES 8 HEARTS

*3 tablespoons butter*
*1 10-ounce package marshmallows*
*6 cups crispy rice cereal*

1. Grease a 15 × 10 × 1-inch baking pan with nonstick spray.
2. In a large saucepan, melt butter over low heat. Add marshmallows and stir until completely melted.
3. Add crispy rice cereal and mix until cereal is well coated.
4. Press mixture evenly into greased baking pan. Let cool slightly.
5. Spray a heart-shaped cookie cutter with nonstick spray and cut crispy treats into heart shapes.

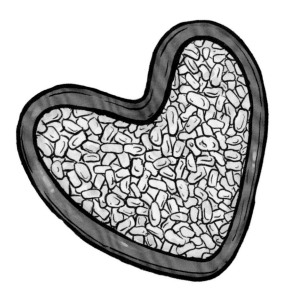

# Pudding Cones

## MAKES 5 SERVINGS

*4 ounces package instant pudding – flavor of your choice*
*1½ cups of milk*
*1 cup cool whip*
*5 flat bottomed ice cream cones*
*Toppings (optional) – whipped cream, nuts, sprinkles, and*
*cherries*

1. Prepare pudding mix with milk as directed on package.
2. Blend in whipped cream topping.
3. Spoon pudding into ice cream cones.
4. On top of pudding add desired toppings.

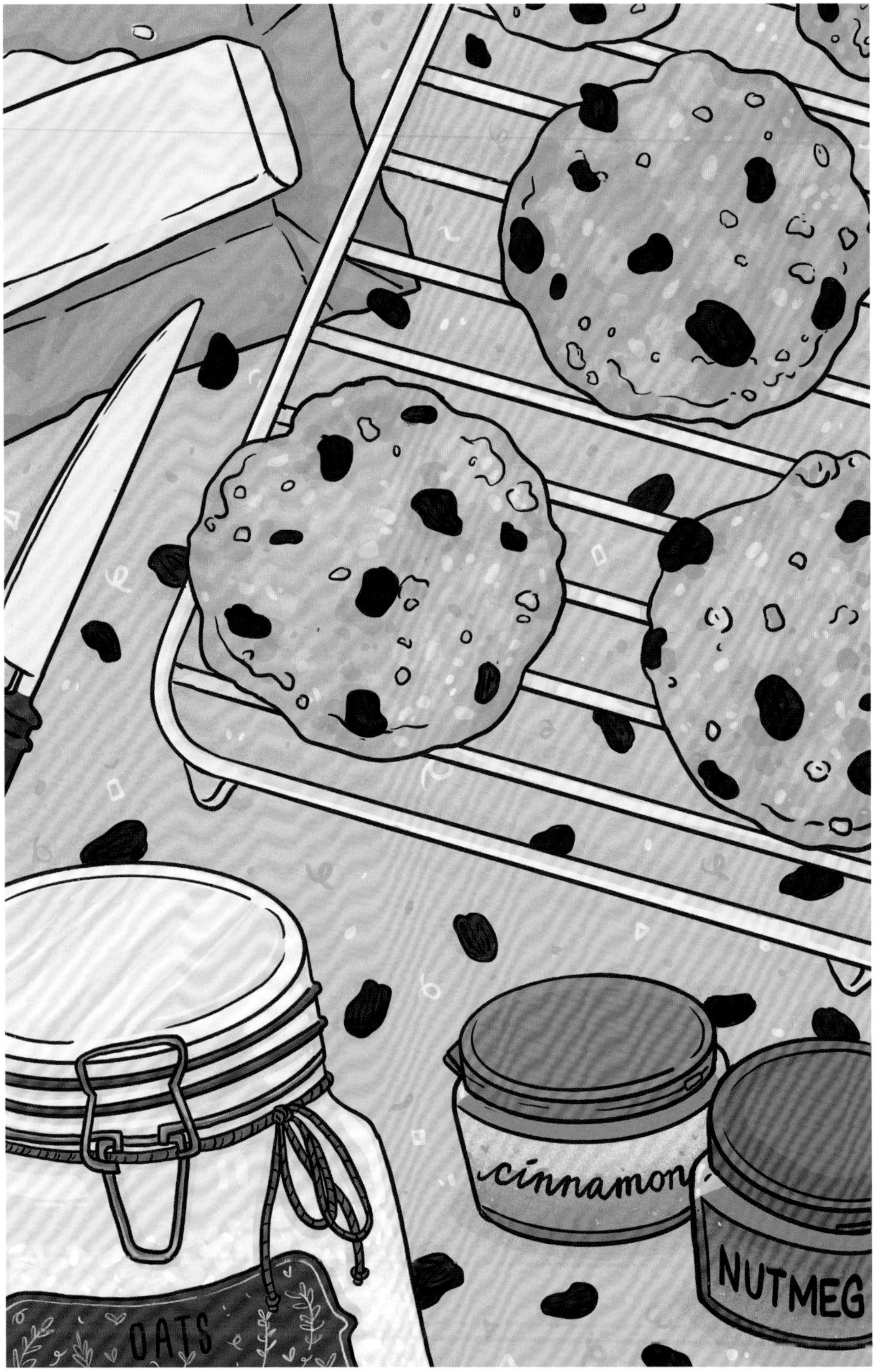
cinnamon
NUTMEG
OATS

# Oatmeal Cinnamon Cookies

MAKES 24 COOKIES

*1 cup unsalted butter, softened*
*1 cup brown sugar, packed*
*½ cup plus 2 tablespoons*
*    granulated sugar*
*2 large eggs*
*1 tablespoon vanilla extract*
*1½ cups all-purpose flour*

*¾ teaspoon salt*
*1 teaspoon baking soda*
*1 teaspoon ground cinnamon*
*½ teaspoon nutmeg, grated*
*1½ cups raisins*
*½ cup walnuts, chopped*
*3 cups rolled oats, not instant*

1. Preheat oven to 350°F. Grease two large cookie sheets or line with Silpat or parchment paper.

2. In a large mixing bowl, beat butter until creamy, add the brown sugar and white sugar, beat until fluffy, about 3 minutes. Beat in eggs, one at a time. Add the vanilla extract.

3. In a medium bowl, mix flour, salt, baking soda, cinnamon, and nutmeg together.

4. Stir the dry ingredients into the butter-sugar mixture. Stir in the raisins, nuts, and oats.

5. Spoon out the dough by large tablespoonfuls onto the prepared cookie sheets, leaving at least 2 inches between each cookie.

6. Bake until the edges of the cookies turn golden brown, about 10 to 12 minutes. Note that the cookies will seem underdone and lightly colored everywhere but the edges. The cookies will firm up as they cool.

7. Cool 1 minute on cookie sheets. Then carefully remove them, using a metal spatula, to a wire rack. Cool completely. They will be quite soft until completely cooled. Store tightly covered.

# Frozen Fruit Ice Pops

## MAKES 6 ICE POPS

*¾ cup plain yogurt*
*2½ cups fruit of your choice—blueberries, cantaloupe, grapes, mango, nectarines, pineapple, peaches, plums, raspberries, strawberries, or watermelon are options.*
*4–5 tablespoons honey*
*¼ teaspoon vanilla extract*
*½ teaspoon lemon juice*

1. Place yogurt, your choice of fruit, and remaining ingredients in a blender in order listed. Blend for 1 minute or until mixture is smooth.

2. Distribute mixture evenly into 6 ice pop molds.

3. Put lids on molds and place in freezer for a minimum of 8 hours.

4. To release an ice pop, run hot water over mold for about 30 seconds.

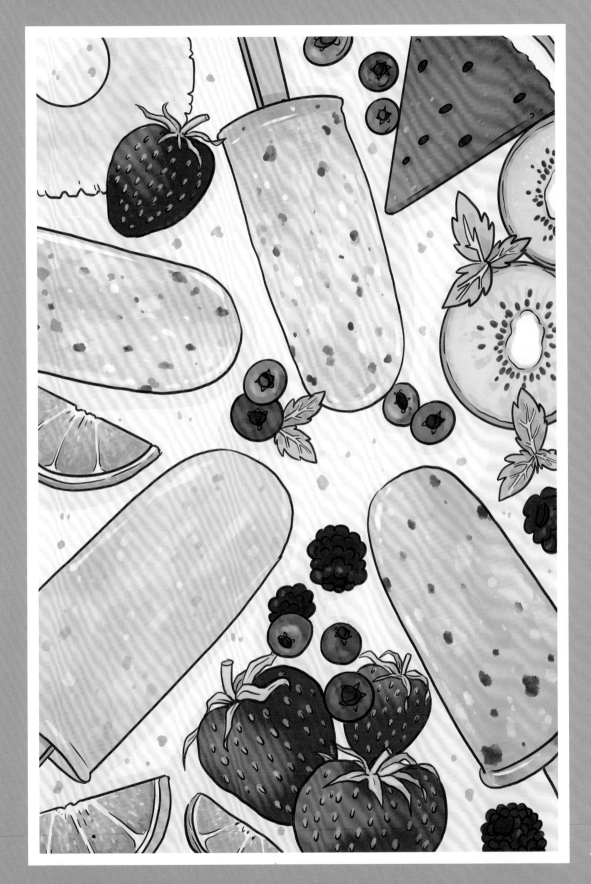

# Chocolate Covered Strawberries

MAKES 10-12 STRAWBERRIES

*10 ounces package high quality bittersweet, semi-sweet, or milk
  chocolate*
*2 pounds fresh strawberries*
*coconut, chopped nuts, and drizzled white chocolate, optional
  toppings*

1.  Line a sheet pan with parchment or waxed paper and set aside.
2.  Start by washing the strawberries and then drying them
    completely. If the strawberries are the least bit wet the chocolate
    will not stick.
3.  If desired, add a handful of toppings, like crushed nuts or coconut,
    onto their own small plates.
4.  Microwave the chocolate for 30 second intervals, removing and
    stirring at each 30 second interval, until the chocolate has melted.
    Stir often, making sure not to burn the chocolate.
5.  Holding a strawberry by the stem, dip into melted chocolate, lift
    and twist slightly, letting the excess chocolate fall back into the
    bowl. At this point you may dip the strawberry in coconut or nuts
    (or leave it plain) and then place the strawberry on the parchment
    paper. Repeat with the rest of the strawberries.
6.  Chill the strawberries until the chocolate sets, about 15 minutes.

# No Bake Peanut Butter Balls

MAKES 16-18 BALLS

*⅓ cup chunky peanut butter*
*¼ cup honey*
*½ teaspoon vanilla extract*
*⅓ cup nonfat dry milk powder*
*⅓ cup quick-cooking oats*
*2 tablespoons graham cracker crumbs*

1. In a small bowl, combine the peanut butter, honey, and vanilla extract. Stir in the milk powder, oats, and graham cracker crumbs. Shape into 1-inch balls. Cover and refrigerate until serving.

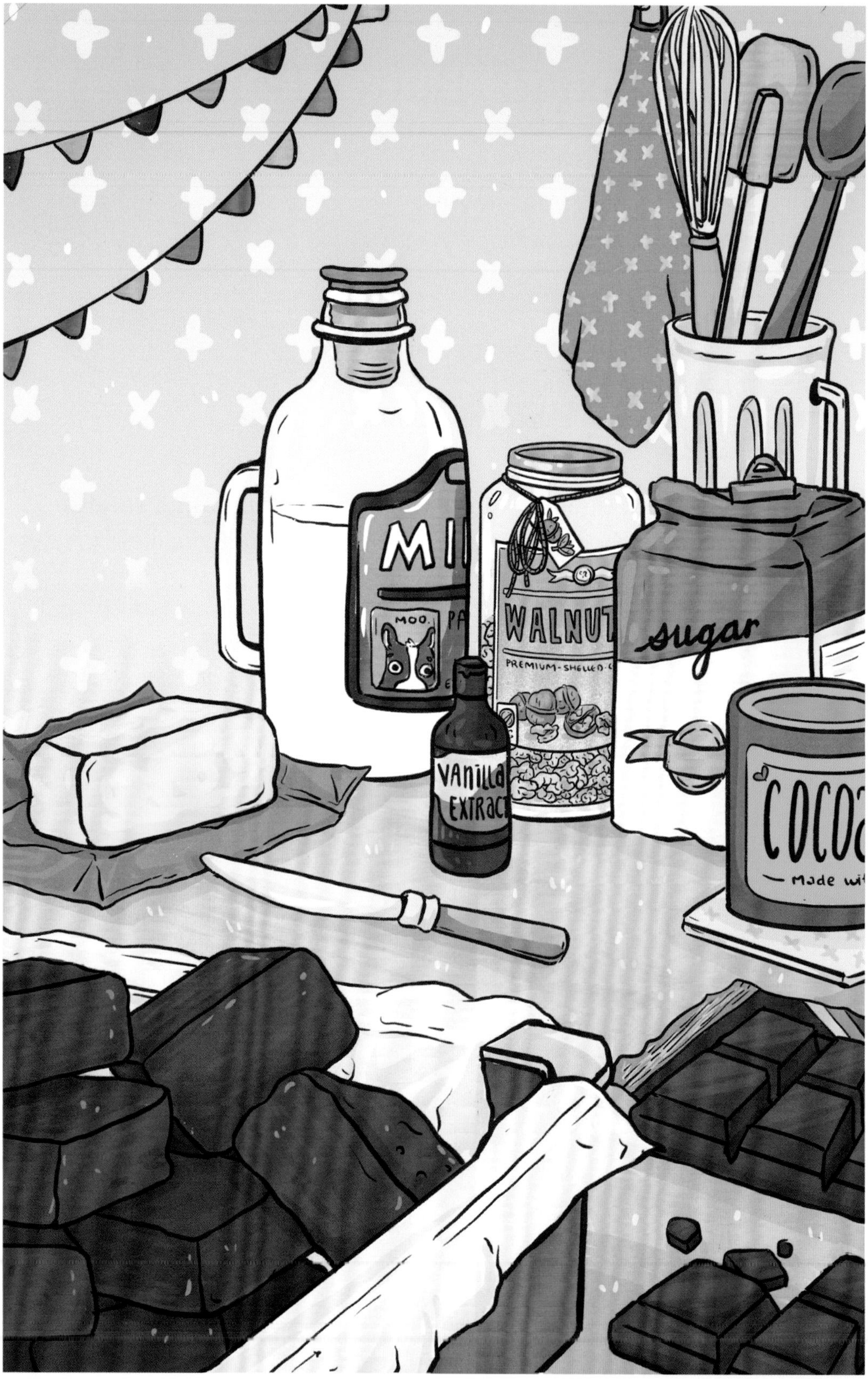
MOO
WALNUT
PREMIUM-SHELLED
sugar
Vanilla

# Chocolate Fudge

MAKES 40 SMALL PIECES

*3 cups semisweet baking chocolate*
*1 14-ounce can sweetened condensed milk*
*2 tablespoons unsweetened cocoa powder*
*2 tablespoons butter*
*1½ teaspoons vanilla extract*
*½ teaspoon salt*
*1 cup walnuts, chopped (optional)*

1. Line an 8 × 8-inch square pan with foil.
2. In a large saucepan, melt together chocolate, sweetened condensed milk, cocoa powder, and butter over medium heat until mixture is completely smooth.
3. Stir in vanilla extract, salt, and chopped nuts (if using).
4. Pour mixture into pan, smoothing to an even layer.
5. Chill in refrigerator for 4 hours, or until firm.
6. Remove foil from pan and cut fudge into squares.

# Cookies on a Stick

## MAKES 20 COOKIES

½ cup butter, softened
½ cup peanut butter
½ cup sugar
½ cup packed brown sugar
1 egg
1 teaspoon vanilla extract
1-½ cups all-purpose flour
½ teaspoon baking powder
½ teaspoon baking soda
20 lollipop sticks
20 miniature Snickers candy bars

1. Preheat oven to 350°F and grease a baking sheet.
2. In a large bowl, cream the butter, peanut butter, sugar, and brown sugar Add the egg and beat well and add in the vanilla extract.
3. In a medium bowl combine the flour, baking powder, and baking soda; gradually add to creamed mixture.
4. Insert a lollipop stick into a side of each candy bar until stick is nearly at the opposite side. Press 1 heaping tablespoon of dough around each candy bar until completely covered. Press dough tightly around the end of the candy bar and the stick.
5. Place cookies 3 in apart on baking sheet and bake for 14 to 16 minutes or until cookies are set. Cool for 1 to 2 minutes before removing from pans to wire racks to cool completely.

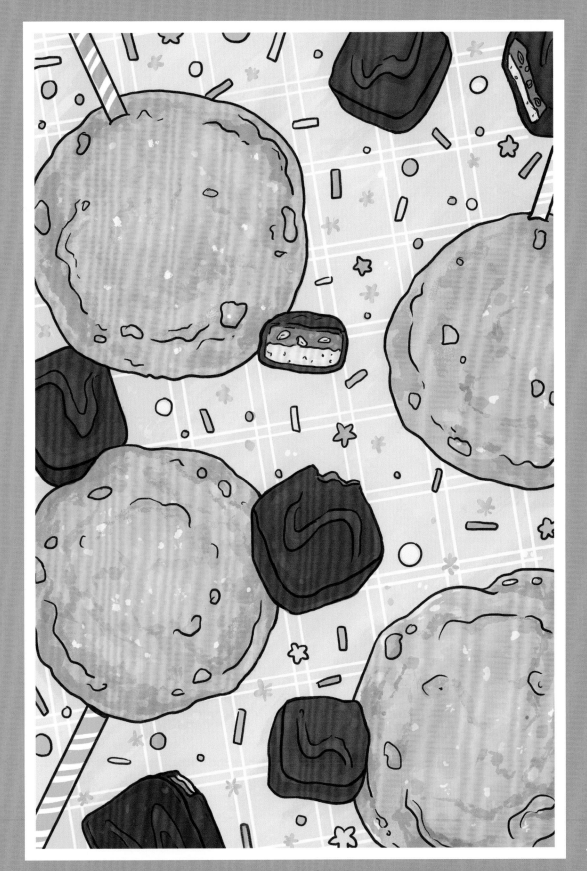

# Soft Pretzels

### MAKES 12 PRETZELS

*1 package active dry yeast*
*1½ cups warm water*
*1 teaspoon salt*
*1 tablespoon sugar*
*3¾–4 cups all-purpose flour*

*1 large egg*
*1 tablespoon water*
*coarse sea salt,*
  *for sprinkling*

1. Preheat oven to 425°F. Line a baking sheet with parchment paper and set aside.

2. Dissolve yeast in warm water, stirring with a spoon for approximately 1 minute; some clumps of yeast may remain. Add salt and sugar and stir until combined. Slowly add 3 cups of flour, one cup at a time, mixing between cups until dough is thick. Add rest of flour until dough is no longer sticky. Dough is ready to knead if it bounces back when poked with your finger.

3. Turn dough out on a flat, floured surface, knead for about 3 minutes, and roll into a ball. With a table knife, cut ball into 12 sections, about one-third cup in size.

4. One at a time, roll each section of dough into a "snake" about 18 to 20 inches long. To shape pretzels, take ends and draw them toward yourself, crossing one over the other to form a loop at top. Cross ends over each other one more time to form a twist, bring ends up to top of loop, and press them down to form a pretzel shape. (See video at www.kitcheninkpublishing/soft pretzel.)

5. In a small bowl, beat egg and 1 tablespoon of water and pour into a shallow bowl. One at a time, dunk each shaped pretzel into egg wash and flip over to cover both sides. Place on a baking sheet and sprinkle with salt.

6. Bake for 10 minutes. Turn oven to broil and bake for 5 more minutes or until tops are browned. Let cool.

# Tiramisu

MAKES 9 SERVINGS

*21 lady finger cookies*
*1 cup chocolate milk*
*1 cup mascarpone*
*1¼ cups whipping cream*
*1½ tablespoons powdered sugar*

## TOPPING

*½ cup chocolate chips*
*2-3 tablespoons unsweetened cocoa powder*

1. In a medium bowl, add mascarpone, whipping cream, and sugar and whip until thick.

2. In a medium bowl, add the chocolate milk and dunk lady fingers on at a time into the milk to coat.

3. Add the coated lady fingers to the bottom of a baking dish (7 ½ x 6 x2 ¼ inches). Each layer should have 7-8 cookies. Spread with ½ of the cream mixture.

4. Sprinkle with chocolate flakes and continue with remaining 1-2 layers. Sprinkle top layer with chocolate flakes and continue with remaining 1-2 layers.

5. Sprinkle top layer with chocolate flakes or dust with cocoa powder just prior to serving. Refrigerate at least 5 hours or overnight before serving.

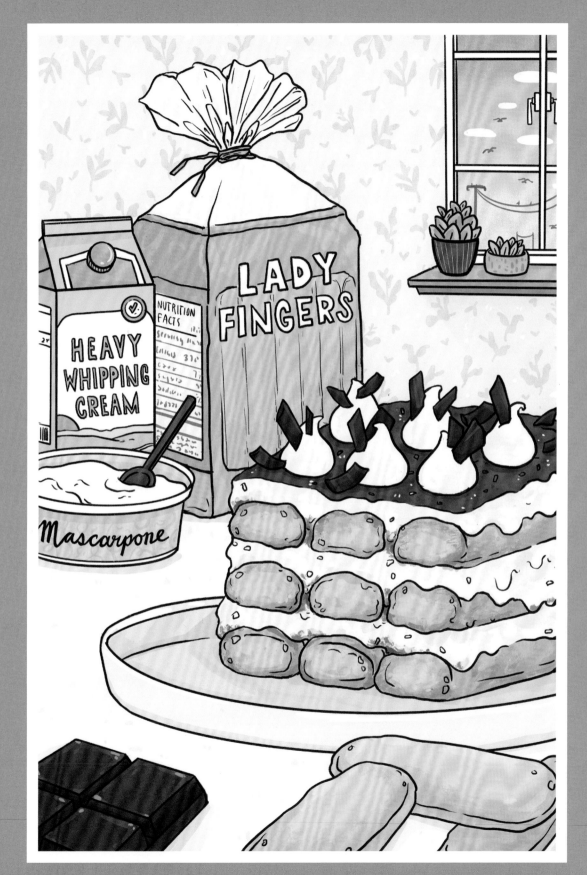

# Chocolate Cupcakes with Chocolate Buttercream Frosting

MAKES 12 CUPCAKES

## CHOCOLATE CUPCAKES
- ¾ cup all-purpose flour
- ½ cup unsweetened cocoa powder
- ¾ teaspoon baking powder
- ½ teaspoon baking soda
- ¼ teaspoon salt
- 2 large eggs
- ½ cup sugar
- ½ cup brown sugar
- ⅓ cup vegetable oil
- 2 teaspoons vanilla extract
- ½ cup buttermilk

## CHOCOLATE BUTTERCREAM FROSTING
- 1 cup (2 sticks) unsalted butter, softened
- 3½ cups confectioners' sugar
- ½ cup unsweetened cocoa powder
- 3 tablespoons heavy cream
- ¼ teaspoon salt
- 2 teaspoons vanilla extract
- sprinkles (optional)

**CUPCAKES**

1. Preheat oven to 350°F. Line a 12-cup muffin tin with cupcake liners.

2. In large bowl, combine flour, cocoa powder, baking powder, baking soda, and salt.

3. In a medium bowl, whisk together eggs, sugar, brown sugar, oil, and vanilla extract until smooth.

4. Pour wet ingredients into dry ingredients and whisk together. Add buttermilk and continue to stir until combined.

5. Fill each cupcake tin two-thirds full.

6. Bake for 18 to 20 minutes, until cupcake is firm to the touch, or a toothpick inserted into center of cupcake comes out clean. Allow to cool completely before frosting.

**FROSTING**

7.  While cupcakes are baking, make frosting. In a large bowl, beat butter until fluffy, about 2 minutes.

8.  Add confectioners' sugar a half cup at a time, beating to combine it after each addition.

9.  Add cocoa powder, heavy cream, salt, and vanilla. Beat on low speed for 30 seconds and then increase to high speed and beat for 1 minute. Frosting should be light and fluffy.

10. Frost cooled cupcakes using a piping bag, butter knife, or small rubber spatula. Top with sprinkles, if desired.

# Watermelon Sorbet

## MAKES 4 SERVINGS

*3½ cups fresh seedless watermelon chunks*
*2 teaspoons lime juice, freshly squeezed*
*¼ cup warm water*
*raw honey (optional)*

1. Line a baking tray with parchment paper and place watermelon chunks on top of parchment. Place in freezer overnight.
2. Remove the watermelon chunks from freezer and blend in a blender, along with lime juice, and allow to sit for 5 minutes to slightly thaw.
3. Blend until smooth and add additional warm water to assist with blending.
4. Eat immediately or freeze in a freezer-safe container for 3 to 4 hours or until firm.

# Raspberry Sorbet

## MAKES 6 SERVINGS

*6 cups raspberries, frozen*
*3 overripe bananas, cut into ½ in pieces frozen*
*fresh raspberries, crushed*

1. In a food processor blend raspberries and bananas until smooth. Divide into three batches to process.
2. Transfer each batch into a large bowl, then stir in crushed raspberries and serve immediately.

# Lemon Bars

MAKES 24 BARS

**SHORTBREAD CRUST**

*1 cup (2 sticks) unsalted butter, melted*
*½ cup sugar*
*2 teaspoons vanilla extract*
*½ teaspoon salt*
*2 cups plus 2 tablespoons all-purpose flour*

**LEMON FILLING**

*2 cups sugar*
*6 tablespoons*
    *all-purpose flour*
*6 large eggs*
*1 cup lemon juice (approximately*
    *4 lemons)*
*confectioners' sugar*

**SHORTBREAD CRUST**

1.  Preheat oven to 325°F and line bottom and sides of a 13 × 9-inch baking pan with parchment paper.

2.  Mix melted butter, sugar, vanilla extract, and salt together in a medium bowl.

3.  Add flour and stir until combined and dough becomes thick.

4.  Press dough firmly and evenly into prepared pan. Bake for 18 to 20 minutes or until edges are lightly browned.

**LEMON FILLING**

1.  Sift sugar and flour together into a large bowl. Add eggs and lemon juice and whisk until completely combined.

2. Pour filling over crust. Bake bars for 25 minutes, or until center is firm.

3. Remove pan from oven, cool 2 hours at room temperature, and then refrigerate for another hour until chilled.

4. Remove from refrigerator and lift up parchment paper to remove from pan.

5. Dust with confectioners' sugar and cut into squares.

# Rainbow Ice Cream

MAKES 8 SERVINGS

*3 cups heavy cream*
*11 ounces sweetened condensed milk*
*1 teaspoon vanilla extract*
*2 drops each color of assorted food coloring – pink, purple, green,*
   *blue, and yellow*
*sprinkles, for topping (optional)*

1. In a large bowl using an electric mixer whisk heavy cream until medium peaks form.
2. Fold in sweetened condensed milk and vanilla and divide into five small bowls.
3. Add a different food coloring into each bowl and stir until combined.
4. Layer spoonful's in a 9 x 5 loaf pan.
5. Smooth the top and run a knife through the mixture to swirl the colors. No more than five swirls as not to overmix.
6. Top with sprinkles and freeze until firm approx. 5 hours.
7. Remove from freezer, let soften, and scoop and serve.

# Cooking Glossary

**AL DENTE:** An Italian term used to describe pasta that is cooked until just slightly firm, meaning "to the tooth" in Italian.

**BAKE:** To cook by dry heat, usually in the oven.

**BASTE:** To moisten food with fat or juices while cooking to add flavor and prevent drying out.

**BATTER:** A mixture containing flour, liquid, and other ingredients. Batter is different from dough because batter is thin enough to pour, while a dough can be formed into a ball and keeps its shape. Batter usually describes unbaked cakes, cookies, or muffins.

**BEAT:** To mix rapidly with a spoon, fork, whisk, or electric mixer to incorporate air and create a smooth, light mixture.

**BLANCH:** To plunge vegetables or fruits into boiling water for a short amount of time, then immerse in an ice water bath to stop the cooking process.

**BLEND:** To combine two or more ingredients thoroughly with a whisk, spoon or mixer until smooth.

**BOIL:** To heat until liquid is so hot bubbles break continually on the surface.

**BRAISE:** To cook meat, fish, or vegetables by first searing in fat, then simmering in liquid over low heat.

**BREAD:** To coat with breadcrumbs, cracker crumbs, or other crumb mixture before cooking.

**BRINE:** A high concentration solution of salt in water. A method for food preservation.

**BROIL:** To cook on a rack under direct heat, usually in an oven.

**BROWN:** To cook over high heat, usually on top of the stove, to brown food.

**BRUSH:** Spread thinly with a brush or with clean fingers.

**CARAMELIZE:** To heat sugar until it liquefies and becomes a golden-brown syrup. Fruits and veggies can also be caramelized.

**CHOP:** To cut food into pieces with a knife, blender, or food processor.

**CHUNKS:** Pieces of food much larger than diced food.

**COMBINE:** Mix ingredients.

**CORE:** To remove the seeds or tough centers from fruits and vegetables.

**CREAM:** Beating butter with sugar until fluffy and creamy.

**CUBE:** Cut into ¼ to ½ inch squares.

**CURDLE:** When the liquid and solid parts of a mixture separate.

**DASH:** A small quantity.

**DEEP FRY:** To cook food by completely immersing it in hot oil or fat.

**DEGLAZE:** To loosen brown bits from the bottom of a pan by adding a liquid, then heating while stirring and scraping the pan.

**DESEED:** To take the seeds out of a fruit or vegetable.

**DICE:** To cut food into small cubes of a consistent size.

**DOLLUP:** A large spoonful of a soft food.

**DOT:** Drop bits of butter or cheese over the entire surface of the food you are cooking.

**DILUTE:** To thin a liquid by adding more liquid to it, usually water or milk.

**DOUGH:** An uncooked mixture of flour, liquid, and other ingredients that creates a firm mixture, usually used to describe bread or cookies. Dough is different from batter because dough can be shaped into a ball, while batter can be poured.

**DRAIN:** Pour off liquid from foods that have been soaked or cooked, either with a mesh strainer or colander.

**DREDGE:** To lightly coat food with flour or breadcrumbs.

**DRIZZLE:** Pouring a liquid over food in a slow, light trickle.

**DRY-FRYING:** Frying without oil or fat.

**DUST:** To decorate cakes and pastries by coating lightly with powdered sugar.

**EMULSIFY:** To combine two or more liquids that do not usually mix into one another – like oil and vinegar. The process involves adding one liquid very slowly into the other and mixing vigorously.

**ENTRÉE:** The main dish.

**FILLET:** To cut the bones from a piece of meat, poultry, or fish. Also, a flat piece of boneless meat, poultry, or fish.

**FOLD:** Mix ingredients with a rubber spatula, whisk, or spoon. Using a gentle over-and-under motion.

**FRY:** To cook food in hot oil or butter until browned or cooked through.

**GARNISH:** Make food look as good as it tastes. To add an edible decoration to make food more attractive.

**GLAZE:** To lightly coat with a glossy substance, which can be either sweet or savory.

**GRATE:** To shred food into tiny pieces by rubbing against a grater

**GREASE:** To coat a pan with butter or oil to prevent food from sticking during baking.

**GRILL:** To cook food over fire or hot coals, usually on a metal frame.

**HULL:** Cutting off the green stalks and leaves of fruit.

**JUICE:** Squeezing the liquid from fruits or vegetables.

**JULIENNE:** To cut food into long, thin strips shaped like matchsticks.

**KNEAD:** To massage dough with the palms of your hands or a machine, continually pressing and folding for several minutes until dough is smooth.

**LINE:** To put nonstick parchment paper or silicone mat into the base of a pan, so that the cake does not stick to it.

**LUKEWARM:** Neither cool nor warm; approximately body temperature.

**MARINATE:** To soak meat, chicken, or fish in a flavored liquid mixture.

**MELT:** Heat until liquid.

**MINCE:** Chop or cut into tiny pieces.

**MIX:** Stir ingredients together.

**MOUND:** Heap food into a mountain shape.

**PAN-FRY:** To cook in a skillet in a small amount of fat.

**PARBOIL:** Boiling for half the normal cooking time to soften, not to completely cook.

**PARE:** Cut away the outside covering of fruits and vegetables.

**PEEL:** To remove the peels from vegetables or fruits.

**PICKLE:** To preserve meats, vegetables, and fruits in brine.

**PINCH:** A pinch is the small amount of an ingredient you can hold between your thumb and forefinger.

**PIT:** Take out the seeds.

**POACH:** To cook very gently in a hot simmering liquid.

**PURÉE:** To blend food together until it becomes completely smooth.

**REDUCE:** To thicken and intensify the flavor of a liquid by boiling it until the liquid reduces in volume, so the flavor is concentrated.

**REST:** To set food aside for a short time, usually to allow a change in texture.

**RIND:** The hard outer edge of cheese or fruit.

**RISING:** The time it takes for the dough to increase in size.

**ROAST:** To cook by dry heat in an oven.

**ROUX:** A thickened paste made from cooked butter and flour, usually used to thicken sauces.

**SCOLD:** Heat milk just below boiling point. Tiny bubbles will form around the edges.

**SAUTÉ:** To cook or brown food in a small amount of hot fat over high heat.

**SCORE:** Making long, shallow cuts in food, to reduce cooking time or allow flavor to be absorbed.

**SEAR:** To brown the surface of meat over high heat to add flavor.

**SEASON:** To flavor meat, fish, or vegetables with salt, pepper, or other seasonings.

**SIFT:** To remove lumps from dry ingredients with a mesh strainer.

**SIMMER:** To heat a liquid over very low heat.

**SLICE:** Cut an ingredient across into pieces that are the same thickness.

**STEAM:** To cook food set above boiling water in a covered pan.

**STEW:** To simmer slowly in a small amount of liquid for a long time.

**STIR:** To mix around and around with a spoon.

**STIR-FRY:** To quickly cook small pieces of food in a small amount of hot oil, stirring constantly.

**STRAIN:** To use a colander to drain liquid from food.

**TOAST:** Browning and crisping food under a broiler, in a toaster, or in the oven.

**TOSS:** To combine ingredients with a gentle, lifting motion.

**TRIM:** Cutting off the unwanted parts of fruit, vegetables, meat, or fish.

**TURNOVER:** Lift the food straight up, then quickly flip it over to the other side.

**WARMING:** Heating gently over a low heat, without boiling.

**WHIP:** To quickly beat ingredients together with a whisk or electric mixer until light and fluffy, like with heavy cream or egg whites. This motion adds air to the ingredients.

**WHISK:** To beat air into ingredients with a fork or whisk to mix or blend.

**ZEST:** To remove the outer part of citrus fruits with a small grater to make zest, which is used as a flavoring.

# Books for Kids Who Love to Cook!

Follow the adventures of Hamish the Hedgehog and create six kid friendly, parent approved yummy recipes in this delightfully entertaining storybook cookbook series.
Find the hidden cat in every book!

*A colorful celebration of food and culture—children will delight in cooking (and eating) their way around the nation. – Kirkus Review*

Take kids on a road trip around the USA without leaving your kitchen. More than 120 delicious recipes, fun facts, and laugh-out-loud jokes are sprinkled throughout, along with 150 colorful illustrations. No suitcase required for this road trip!

www.kitcheninkpublishing.com